Storybook Cross-Stitch

by The Vanessa-Ann Collection

Storybook Cross-Stitch

by The Vanessa-Ann Collection

Meredith® Press
New York, New York

Meredith® Press is an imprint of Meredith® Books:
President, Book Group: Joseph J. Ward
Vice President, Editorial Director: Elizabeth P. Rice
For Meredith® Press:
Executive Editor: Maryanne Bannon
Senior Editor: Carol Spier
Associate Editor: Ruth Weadock
Production Manager: Bill Rose

For Chapelle Ltd.:
Owner: Jo Packham
Staff: Sandra Anderson, Malissa Boatwright, Trice Boerens, Rebecca Christensen, Holly Fuller,
Cherie Hanson, Holly Hollingsworth, Susan Jorgensen, Susan Laws, Amanda McPeck,
Tammy Perkins, Jamie Pierce, Leslie Ridenour, Edie Stockstill, Amy Vineyard,
Nancy Whitley, and Lorrie Young

Photographers: Ryne Hazen, Kevin Dilley
Framing: Artist's Touch

ISBN: 0-696-02385-7 (hardcover)
ISBN: 0-696-20436-3 (softcover)
Library of Congress Catalog Card Number: 93-086665
First Printing 1995

Distributed by Meredith Corporation, Des Moines, IA
10 9 8 7 6 5 4 3 2 1
Printed in the United States of America.

Dear Crafter,

Storybook Cross-Stitch is filled with fantastical images and faraway lands, memorable characters and lasting messages. Whether it's Androcles' kindness to the lion or Cinderella's happily-ever-after ending, these stories and poems are an integral part of childhood "quiet times," fond memories in the making for our grown-up years. Here, they are captured in cross-stitch forever, in designs both beautiful and whimsical, appealing to young and old alike.

Whichever projects you choose for displaying at home or giving as wonderful hand-crafted gifts, we've provided full-color photographs, easy-to-read color charts, and complete step-by-step directions for each piece. There are even helpful sewing and stitching Basics sections for your reference, plus a handy Suppliers list for materials and tools.

We hope you enjoy creating these delightful keepsakes as much as we enjoyed bringing them to you.

Sincerely,

Ruth Weadock

Ruth Weadock
Associate Editor

Introduction

The nursery rhymes, fairy tails and fables you cherished as a child have been the favorites of both parents and children for hundreds of years. Countless readings of these timeless tales have bonded generations together as young ones sit on laps memorizing verses, giggling at the character voices, and discussing "the moral of the story."

Now you can pass on a token of these treasured moments with twenty-five beautiful designs by the artists of the Vanessa-Ann Collection. Each captures the magic of those special memories with the heirloom quality and personal touch only achieved in cross-stitch. These finished pieces will be keepsakes which, like the stories that inspired them, will be shared by future generations.

Jo Packham

Jo Packham
Owner, The Vanessa-Ann Collection

Contents

Fairy Tales..8

Little Red Ridinghood..10

Goldilocks and the Three Bears................................16

Hansel and Gretel..22

The Frog Prince...28

The Princess and the Pea...34

Cinderella...40

Rapunzel..46

Rumplestiltskin...52

Nursery Rhymes..58

Hey Diddle Diddle, the Cat and the Fiddle.................60

...The Cow Jumped Over the Moon...........................64

Ring A Ring O Roses...66

Rock-a-Bye Baby..74

Jack Sprat..82

Little Bo Peep...88

Twinkle, Twinkle Little Star..94

Mary, Mary, Quite Contrary......................................100

The Old Woman Who Lived in a Shoe.......................106

Fables 114

The Goose that Laid the Golden Egg 116

The Wind and the Sun 122

A Wolf in Sheep's Clothing 128

The Tortoise and the Hare 132

The Country Mouse and City Mouse 136

Androcles and the Lion 144

The Fisherman and His Wife 150

The Leopard and the Fox 156

General Instructions for Cross-Stitch 164

General Instructions for Pillows 166

Suppliers 167

Index 168

Fairy

Rapunzel

The Frog Prince

Cinderella

Tales

Little Red Riding Hood

The Princess and the Pea

Rumpelstiltskin

Goldilocks and The Three Bears

Hansel and Gretel

Little Red Ridinghood

. . . The Wolf walked with Little Red Ridinghood for a time, then said, "Look at the pretty roses! It is such a lovely day, I'm sure your grandmother would be pleased if you spent some time to gather some for her."

Little Red Ridinghood thought, "It is still early in the morning. I will have plenty of time to pick them." So she left the path and wandered deeper into the woods to pick flowers.

In the meantime the Wolf left her and ran straight off to her grandmother's cottage . . .

Little Red Ridinghood

SAMPLE

Stitched on Sand Belfast Linen 32 over two threads, the finished design size is 6⅜" x 9¼". The fabric was cut 13" x 16". Frame as desired.

Other Fabrics	Finished Design
Aida 11	9¼" x 13⅜"
Aida 14	7¼" x 10½"
Aida 18	5⅝" x 8⅛"
Hardanger 22	4⅝" x 6⅝"

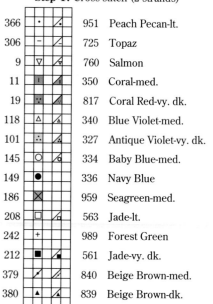

Anchor			DMC (used for sample)	
Step 1: Cross-stitch (2 strands)				
366	·		951	Peach Pecan-lt.
306	−		725	Topaz
9	▽		760	Salmon
11	I		350	Coral-med.
19			817	Coral Red-vy. dk.
118	△		340	Blue Violet-med.
101			327	Antique Violet-vy. dk.
145	O		334	Baby Blue-med.
149	●		336	Navy Blue
186	✕		959	Seagreen-med.
208	□		563	Jade-lt.
242	+		989	Forest Green
212	■		561	Jade-vy. dk.
379	╱		840	Beige Brown-med.
380	▲		839	Beige Brown-dk.

Step 2: Backstitch (1 strand)

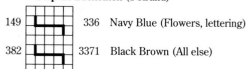

149	336	Navy Blue (Flowers, lettering)
382	3371	Black Brown (All else)

Top left • Stitch Count: 103 x 147

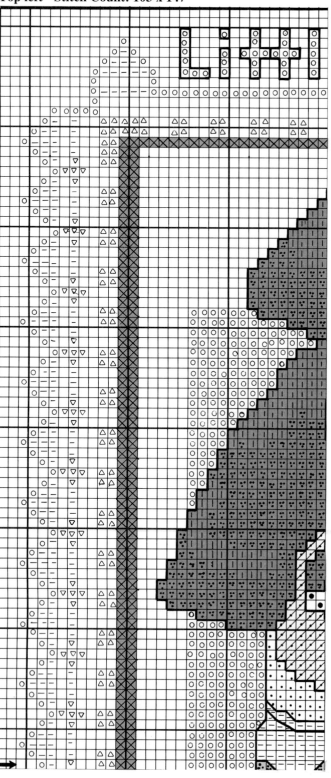

12

13

Little Red Ridinghood

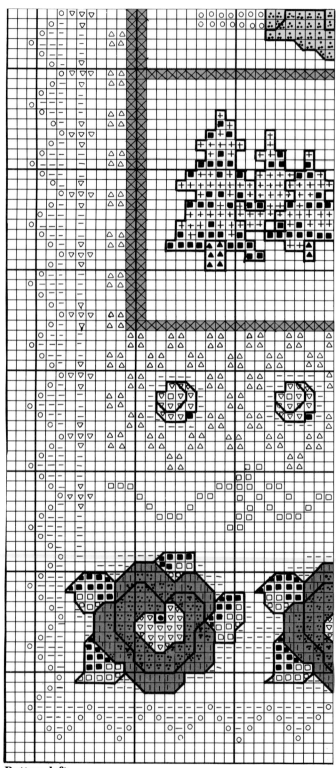

Bottom left

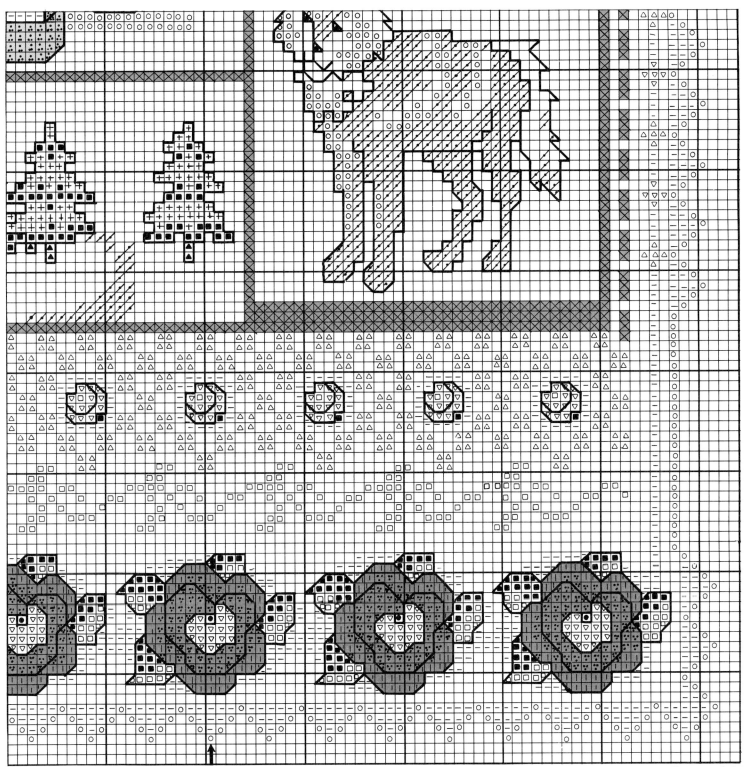

Bottom right

... One day, after the bears had made porridge for their breakfast, they walked out into the woods while the porridge was cooling. While they were walking, a little girl named Goldilocks came to the house. She peeped in the keyhole and then looked in the window where she saw the porridge. If she had been a thoughtful little girl, she might have waited until the bears returned, and perhaps they would have invited her to breakfast. But the porridge was tempting, and she opened the door so she could help herself ...

The Story of the Three Bears

nce upon a time there were three bears wh... house in...

Goldilocks and

The Three Bears

Goldilocks and the Three Bears

SAMPLE
Stitched on Cream Murano 30 over two
threads, the finished design size is 7⅝" x 10¼".
The fabric was cut 13" x 16". Frame as
desired.

Other Fabrics   **Finished Design**
Aida 11   10⅜" x 14"
Aida 14   8⅛" x 11"
Aida 18   6⅜" x 8½"
Hardanger 22   5⅛" x 7"

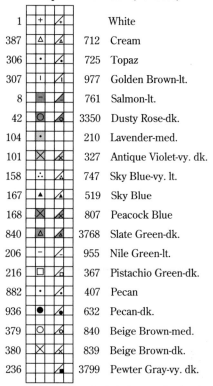

Anchor			DMC	(used for sample)
Step 1: Cross-stitch (2 strands)				
1	+	⁄		White
387	△	⁄	712	Cream
306	·	⁄	725	Topaz
307	‖	⁄	977	Golden Brown-lt.
8	▬	⁄	761	Salmon-lt.
42	○	⁄	3350	Dusty Rose-dk.
104	·		210	Lavender-med.
101	✕	⁄	327	Antique Violet-vy. dk.
158	∴	⁄	747	Sky Blue-vy. lt.
167	▲	⁄	519	Sky Blue
168	✕	⁄	807	Peacock Blue
840	△	⁄	3768	Slate Green-dk.
206	–	⁄	955	Nile Green-lt.
216	□	⁄	367	Pistachio Green-dk.
882	·	⁄	407	Pecan
936	●	⁄	632	Pecan-dk.
379	○	⁄	840	Beige Brown-med.
380	✕	⁄	839	Beige Brown-dk.
236	■	⁄	3799	Pewter Gray-vy. dk.

Step 2: Backstitch (1 strand)

| 236 | | 3799 | Pewter Gray-vy. dk. |

Step 3: French Knot (1 strand)

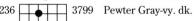

| 236 | ● | 3799 | Pewter Gray-vy. dk. |

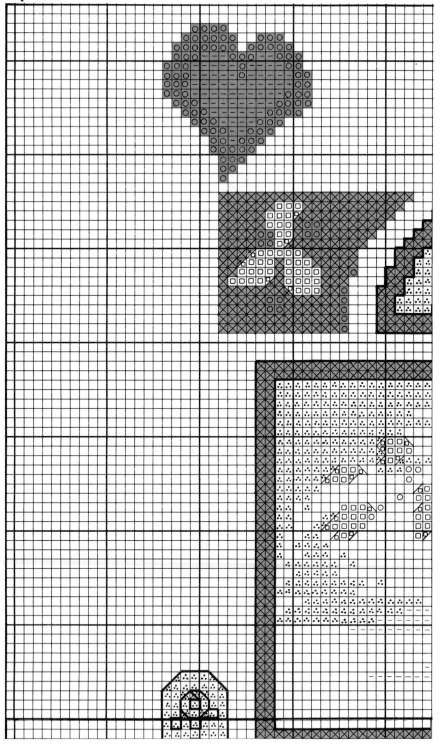

Top left • Stitch Count: 114 x 154

Goldilocks and the Three Bears

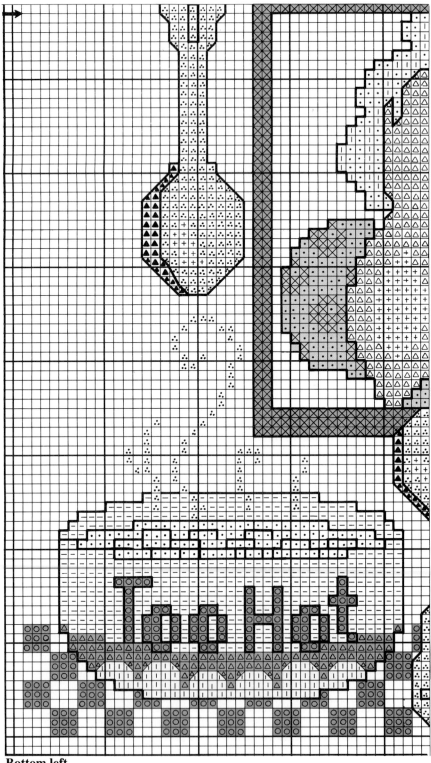

Bottom left

just right

. . . They searched but they found no crumbs, for the birds had eaten them all. But a snow-white bird led them to a cottage made of gingerbread which was covered with candy and cakes. By this time, Hansel and Gretel were quite hungry.

"We can have a real feast now," said Hansel, not knowing of the evil witch who lurked inside . . .

Hansel and Gretel

Hansel and Gretel

SAMPLE
Stitched on Antique White Murano 30 over two threads, the finished design size is 9¾" x 7⅞". The fabric was cut 16" x 14". Frame as desired.

Other Fabrics	Finished Design
Aida 11	13⅜" x 10⅞"
Aida 14	10½" x 8½"
Aida 18	8⅛" x 6⅝"
Hardanger 22	6⅝" x 5⅜"

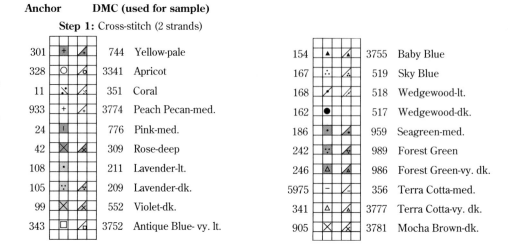

Anchor		DMC (used for sample)	
Step 1: Cross-stitch (2 strands)			
301		744	Yellow-pale
328		3341	Apricot
11		351	Coral
933		3774	Peach Pecan-med.
24		776	Pink-med.
42		309	Rose-deep
108		211	Lavender-lt.
105		209	Lavender-dk.
99		552	Violet-dk.
343		3752	Antique Blue- vy. lt.
154		3755	Baby Blue
167		519	Sky Blue
168		518	Wedgewood-lt.
162		517	Wedgewood-dk.
186		959	Seagreen-med.
242		989	Forest Green
246		986	Forest Green-vy. dk.
5975		356	Terra Cotta-med.
341		3777	Terra Cotta-vy. dk.
905		3781	Mocha Brown-dk.

Top left • Stitch Count: 147 x 119

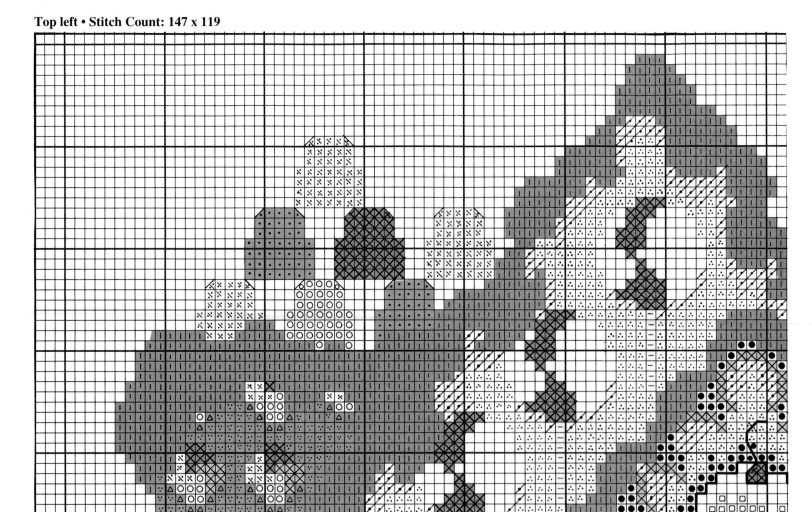

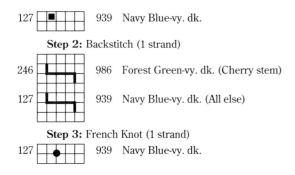

127 | ■ | 939 Navy Blue-vy. dk.

Step 2: Backstitch (1 strand)

246 | 986 Forest Green-vy. dk. (Cherry stem)

127 | 939 Navy Blue-vy. dk. (All else)

Step 3: French Knot (1 strand)

127 | ● | 939 Navy Blue-vy. dk.

Top right

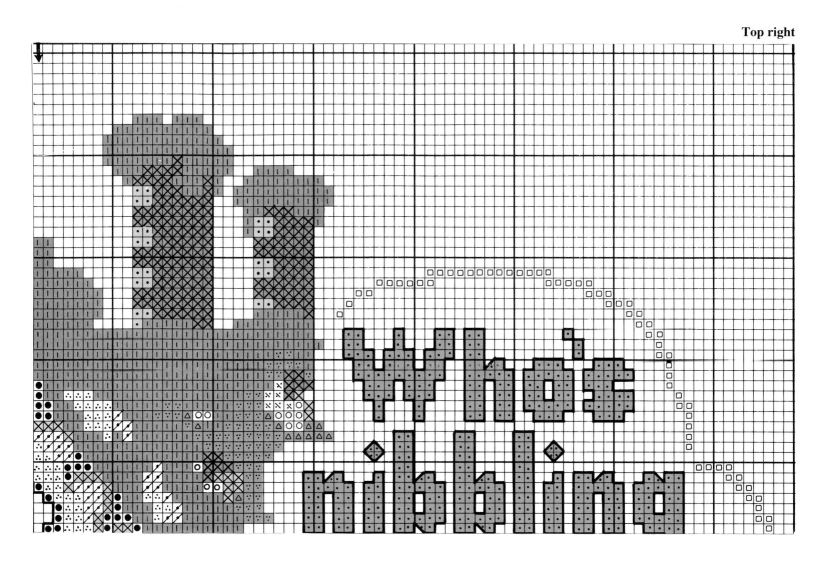

Hansel and Gretel

Bottom left

Bottom right

The Frog Prince

THE FROG PRINCE

"You see, I wasn't what I seemed to be," he said. "An evil woman cast a spell on me that no one but you could break."

She could say nothing as she gazed at the boy prince who had been a large, ugly frog only moments earlier.

"Will you let me be your playmate now?" he asked.

The Princess laughed, and they ran outside together to play with her gold ball, now as the best of friends.

The Frog Prince

SAMPLE
Stitched on Platinum Belfast Linen 32 over two
threads, the finished design size is 10" x 7".
The fabric was cut 17" x 13". Frame as desired.

Other Fabrics	Finished Design
Aida 11	14⅝" x 10⅛"
Aida 14	11½" x 8"
Aida 18	9" x 6¼"
Hardanger 22	7⅜" x 5⅛"

The color key is found on page 32.

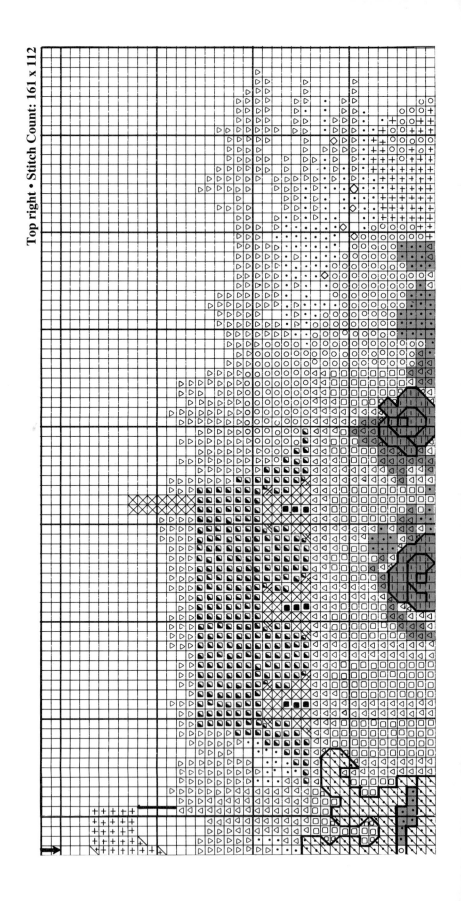

Top right • Stitch Count: 161 x 112

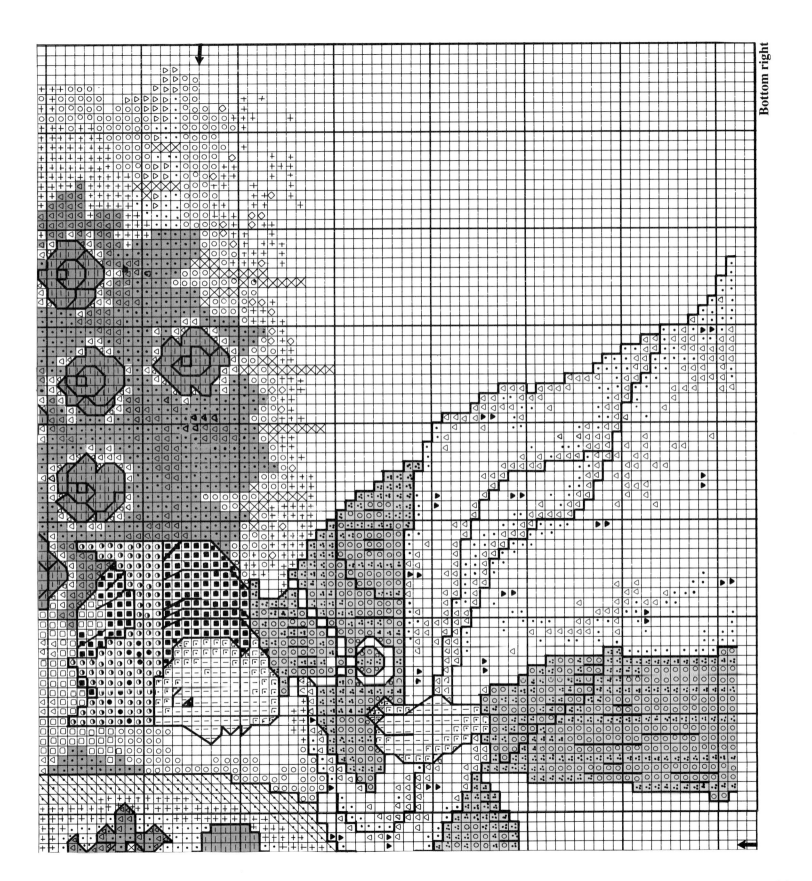

The Frog Prince

Anchor   DMC (used for sample)

Step 1: Cross-stitch (2 strands)

293	727	Topaz-vy. lt.
306	725	Topaz
366	951	Peach Pecan-lt.
881	945	Peach Beige
48	818	Baby Pink
74	3354	Dusty Rose-vy. lt.
76	3731	Dusty Rose-med.
95	554	Violet-lt.
99	552	Violet-dk.
159	3325	Baby Blue-lt.
168	518	Wedgewood-lt.
162	517	Wedgewood-dk.
264	772	Pine Green-lt.
203	564	Jade-vy. lt.
843	3364	Pine Green
861	3363	Pine Green-med.
376	842	Beige Brown-vy. lt.
882	3773	Pecan-vy. lt.
379	840	Beige Brown-med.
309	435	Brown-vy. lt.
351	400	Mahogany-dk.
381	838	Beige Brown-vy. dk.
8581	647	Beaver Gray-med.
273	3787	Brown Gray-dk.
403	310	Black

Step 2: Backstitch (1 strand)

| 306 | 725 | Topaz (Roses) |
| 403 | 310 | Black (All else) |

Step 3: Beads

| | 62012 | Royal Plumb |

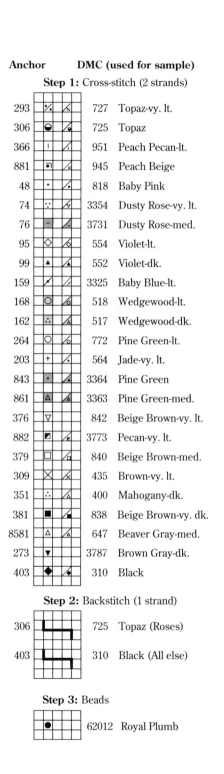

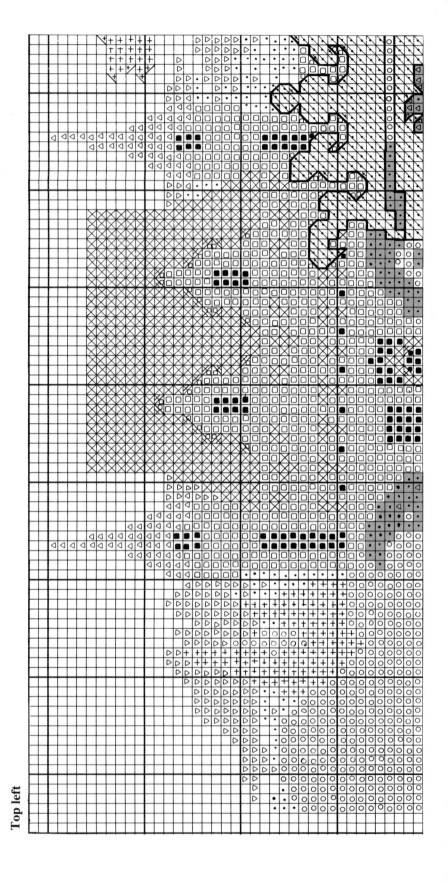

Top left

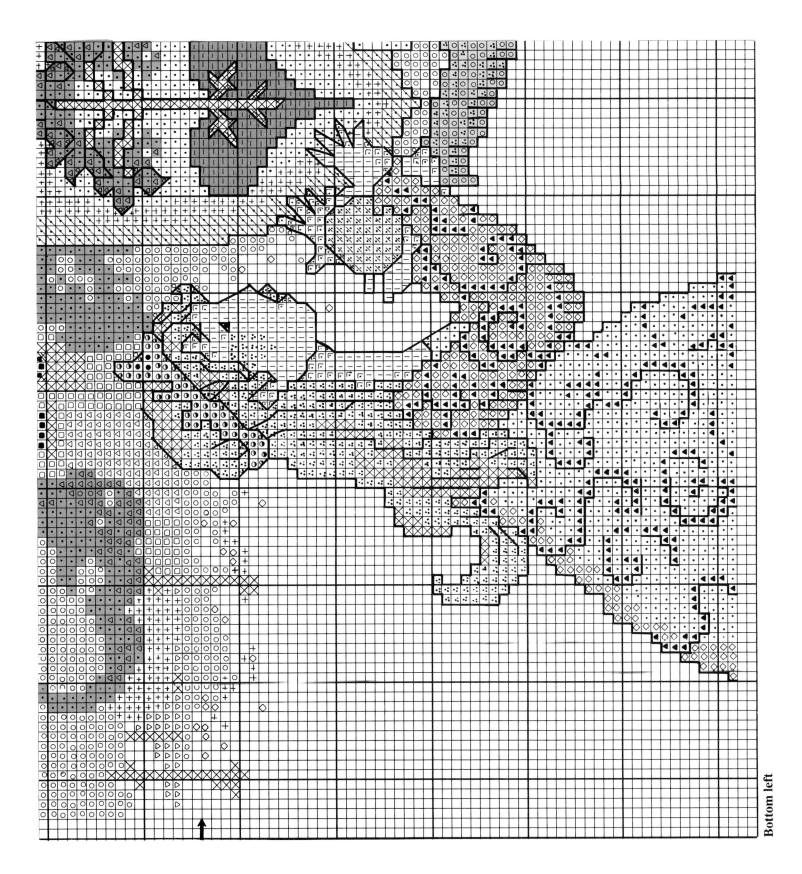

The Princess

. . . The Queen laid twenty mattresses on top of the pea and twenty quilts on top of the mattresses.

"Now we shall see if she is a true princess," she told the king.

The next morning the Queen asked the Princess how she had slept.

"Very badly," she replied. "I slept on something so hard my whole body is black and blue."

Then they knew she was a true princess as she had claimed . . .

and the Pea

The Princess and the Pea

SAMPLE
Stitched on Delicate Teal Jobelan 28 over two
threads, the finished design size is 5⅞" x 11¼".
The fabric was cut 13" x 18". As shown, pillow
measures 21" x 14".

Other Fabrics	Finished Design
Aida 11	7½" x 14¼"
Aida 14	5⅞" x 11¼"
Aida 18	4⅝" x 8¾"
Hardanger 22	3¾" x 7⅛"

The color key is found on page 38.

Pillow Materials

• ½ yard of light pink fabric
• 1 yard of light blue printed fabric
• ⅛ yard of teal fabric
• ½ yard of periwinkle fabric for piping
• ½ yard of paper-backed fusible web
• Matching thread
• Polyester stuffing
• 1 yard of ¼"-diameter cable cord for piping
• 2 yards of ⅜"-diameter cable cord for piping
• Small green button

Pillow Directions

All seams ½" except where noted.

1. Referring to photo for placement, sew button onto stitched piece. With completed design centered, trim stitched piece to 9½" x 14½". From periwinkle fabric, make 1 yard of ¼"-diameter piping (see General Instructions on bias strips and piping). Cut into two 15" pieces. Sew strips to each long side of completed cross-stitch.

2. Cut two pieces of print fabric 28" x 4½". Gather both long edges of each piece until each is 14" long. Cut two 14½" x 2½" pieces each of light pink and teal fabric. Sew one of each color to opposite long edges of each gathered piece. Sew light pink edges to long sides of completed cross-stitch.

3. Cut a 20" x 14½" piece of fusible web. Fuse to wrong side of pillow front following manufacturer's instructions.

4. From periwinkle fabric, make 2 yards of ⅜"-diameter piping. Sew to front of pillow.

5. From light pink fabric, cut a 22" x 15" piece for pillow back. Sew to pillow front (see General Instructions on finishing pillows). Turn right side out; stuff; slipstitch closed.

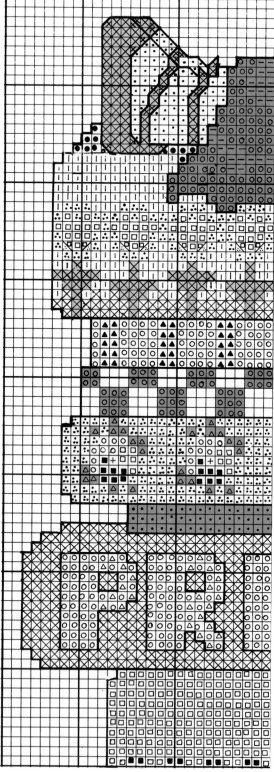

The Princess and the Pea

Anchor   DMC (used for sample)

Step 1: Cross-stitch (2 strands)

Anchor			DMC	(used for sample)
1	△			White
306	∴	◿	725	Topaz
48	ı	◿	818	Baby Pink
893	●	◢	224	Shell Pink-lt.
10	▲		352	Coral-lt.
11	▪		3328	Salmon-dk.
42	▬	◢	335	Rose
59	◎	◿	326	Rose-vy. dk.
118	□	◿	340	Blue Violet-med.
119	■	◣	333	Blue Violet-dk.
185	✕		964	Seagreen-lt.
154	○		3755	Baby Blue
978	⊠	◪	322	Navy Blue-vy. lt.
878	△	◿	501	Blue Green-dk.
885	·	◿	739	Tan-ultra vy. lt.
882	ı	◿	407	Pecan
936	∴	◿	632	Pecan-dk.
382	+		3021	Brown Gray-vy. dk.

Step 2: Backstitch (1 strand)

382	▃	3021	Brown Gray-vy. dk.

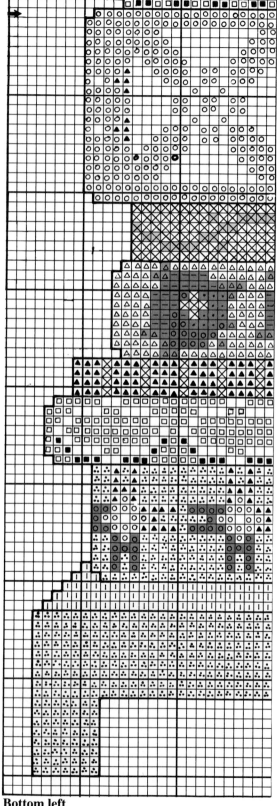

Bottom left

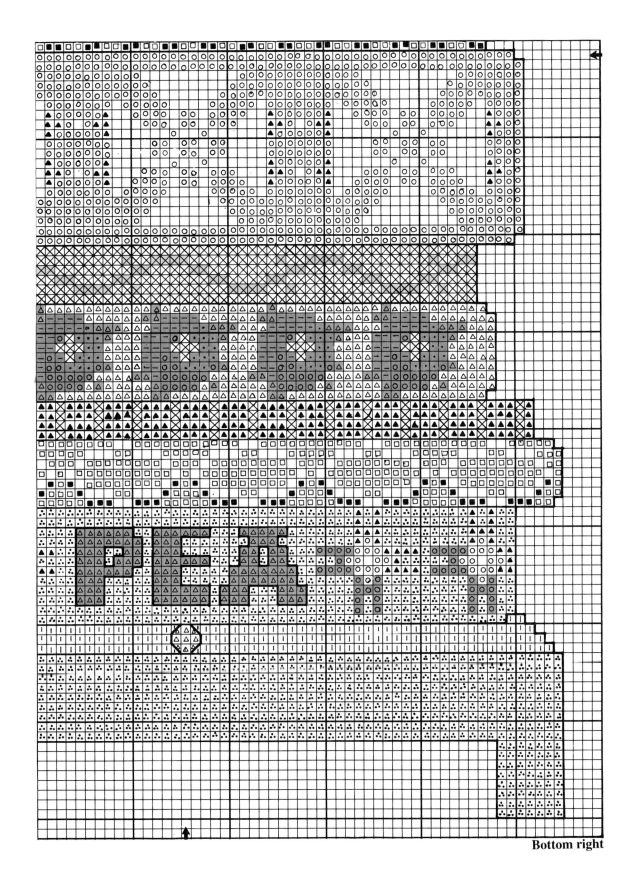

Bottom right

Cinderella

. . . He asked Cinderella to sit. Putting the slipper to her foot, he was astonished to find it went on easily. The surprise of her sisters was great, but was still greater when Cinderella pulled out of her pocket the second slipper.

The Prince courted Cinderella for a few days afterward and found her even more charming than before. Soon they were married, and they lived happily ever after . . .

Cinderella

SAMPLE

Stitched on White Murano 30 over two
threads, the finished design size is 9½" x 8¼".
The fabric was cut 16" x 15". Frame as
desired.

Other Fabrics	Finished Design
Aida 11	12⁷⁄₈" x 11¼"
Aida 14	10⅛" x 8⁷⁄₈"
Aida 18	7⁷⁄₈" x 6⁷⁄₈"
Hardanger 22	6½" x 5⅝"

Anchor			DMC (used for sample)	
			Step 1: Cross-stitch (2 strands)	
386	I	╱	746	Off White
366	+	╱	951	Peach Pecan-lt.
891	⊠	╱	676	Old Gold-lt.
323	·	╱	722	Orange Spice-lt.
326	∴	╱	720	Orange Spice-dk.
892	□	╱	225	Shell Pink-vy. lt.
893	◇	╱	224	Shell Pink-lt.
74	⊙	╱	3354	Dusty Rose-vy. lt.
69	⁚	╱	3687	Mauve

Top left • Stitch Count: 142 x 124

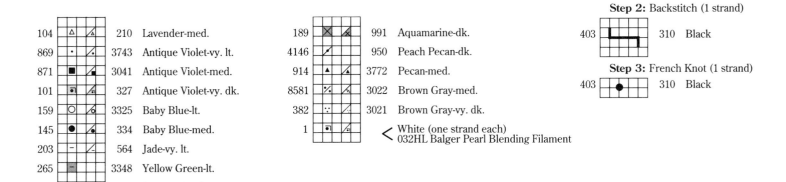

104	△ ◢	210	Lavender-med.	189	⊠ ◪	991	Aquamarine-dk.
869	· ◿	3743	Antique Violet-vy. lt.	4146	◹	950	Peach Pecan-dk.
871	■ ◣	3041	Antique Violet-med.	914	▲ ◿	3772	Pecan-med.
101	▣ ◢	327	Antique Violet-vy. dk.	8581	◿	3022	Brown Gray-med.
159	○ ◔	3325	Baby Blue-lt.	382	∵ ◿	3021	Brown Gray-vy. dk.
145	● ◖	334	Baby Blue-med.	1	▣ ◿		White (one strand each)
203	–	564	Jade-vy. lt.				032HL Balger Pearl Blending Filament
265	▦	3348	Yellow Green-lt.				
186	▽ ◿	993	Aquamarine-lt.				

Step 2: Backstitch (1 strand)

403	⌐	310	Black

Step 3: French Knot (1 strand)

403	●	310	Black

Top right

Cinderella

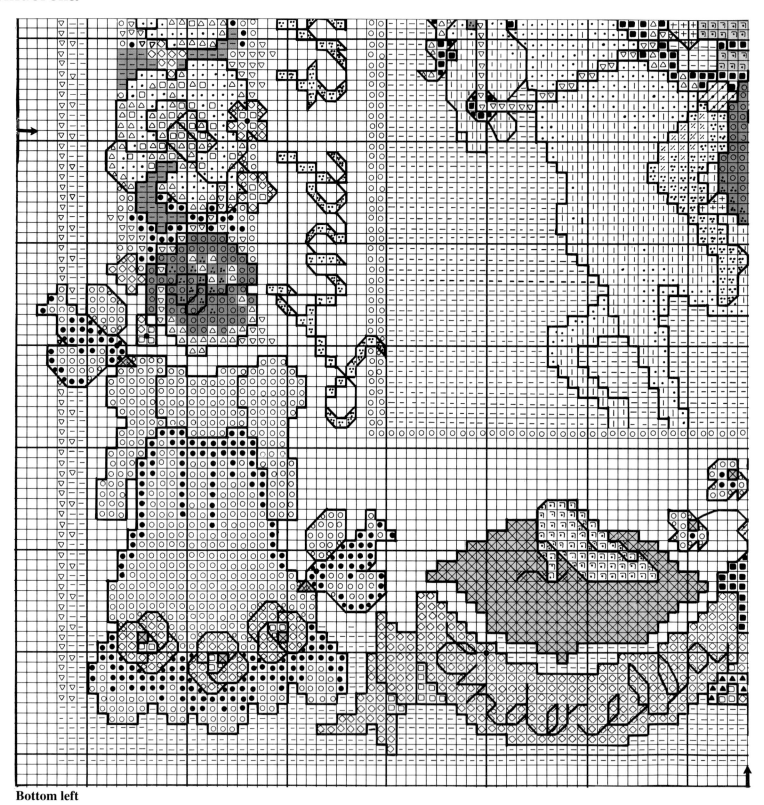

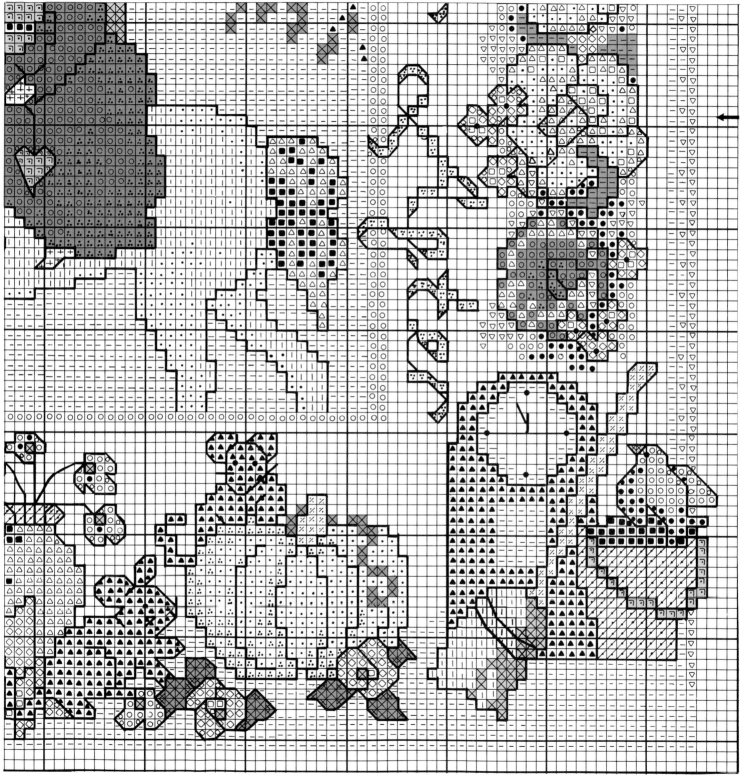

Bottom right

Rapunzel

... The Prince had heard Rapunzel's voice, but searched in vain for a door to the tower. Then one day, as he hid behind a tree, he heard the Witch call out:

Rapunzel, Rapunzel, let down your golden hair.

"So that is the way up," the Prince said. "Then I will climb up, too, and visit the maiden ..."

Rapunzel

SAMPLE
Stitched on Pewter Murano 30 over two threads, the finished design size is 6½" x 8⅜". The fabric was cut 13" x 15".

Other Fabrics	Finished Design
Aida 11	8⅞" x 11⅜"
Aida 14	6⅞" x 8⅞"
Aida 18	5⅜" x 7
Hardanger 22	4⅜" x 5⅝"

Tray
The tray shown is made from a picture frame with a mat, glass, sturdy backing, and handles. The mat opening is about 7" x 8¾". For best results, have it framed by a professional framer.

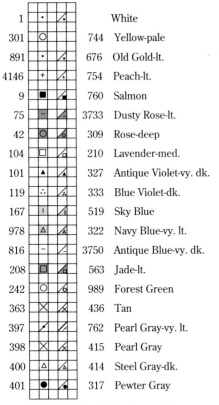

Anchor		DMC (used for sample)	
Step 1: Cross-stitch (2 strands)			
1			White
301		744	Yellow-pale
891		676	Old Gold-lt.
4146		754	Peach-lt.
9		760	Salmon
75		3733	Dusty Rose-lt.
42		309	Rose-deep
104		210	Lavender-med.
101		327	Antique Violet-vy. dk.
119		333	Blue Violet-dk.
167		519	Sky Blue
978		322	Navy Blue-vy. lt.
816		3750	Antique Blue-vy. dk.
208		563	Jade-lt.
242		989	Forest Green
363		436	Tan
397		762	Pearl Gray-vy. lt.
398		415	Pearl Gray
400		414	Steel Gray-dk.
401		317	Pewter Gray
Step 2: Backstitch (1 strand)			
236		3799	Pewter Gray-vy. dk.

Top left • Stitch Count: 97 x 125

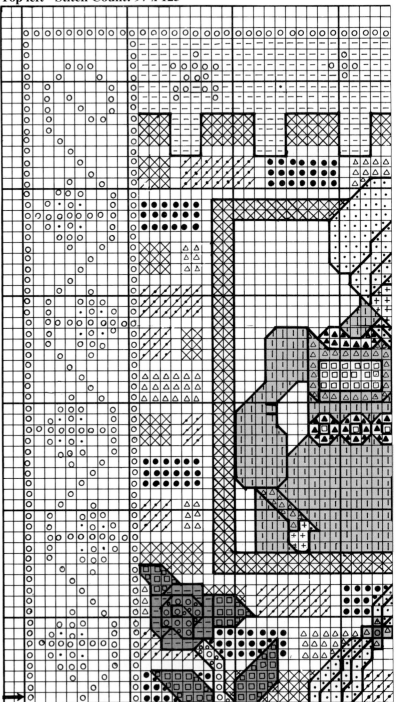

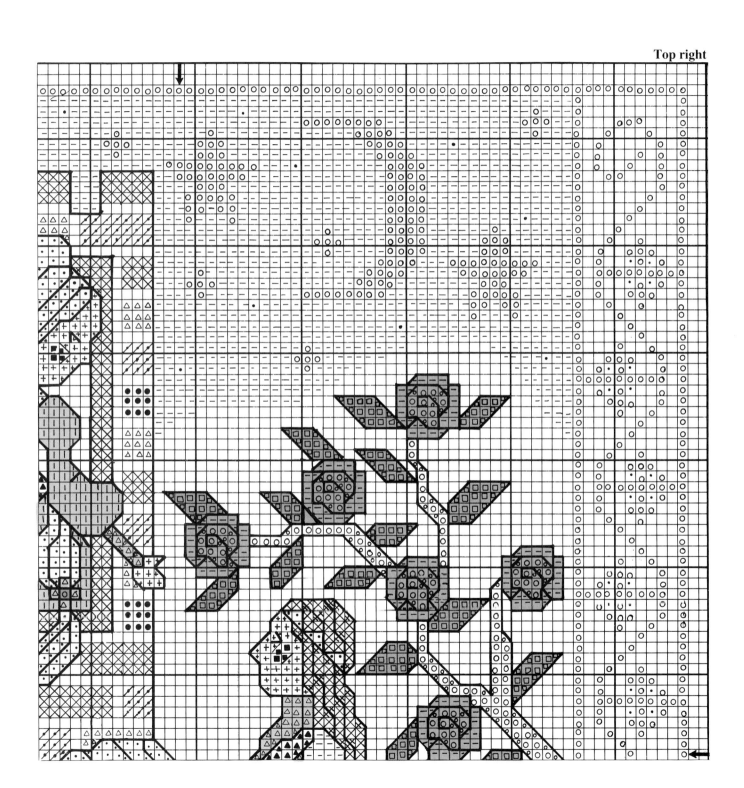

Rapunzel

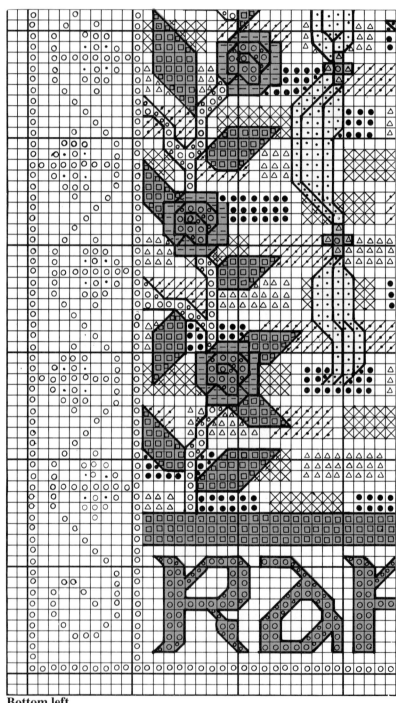

Bottom left

50

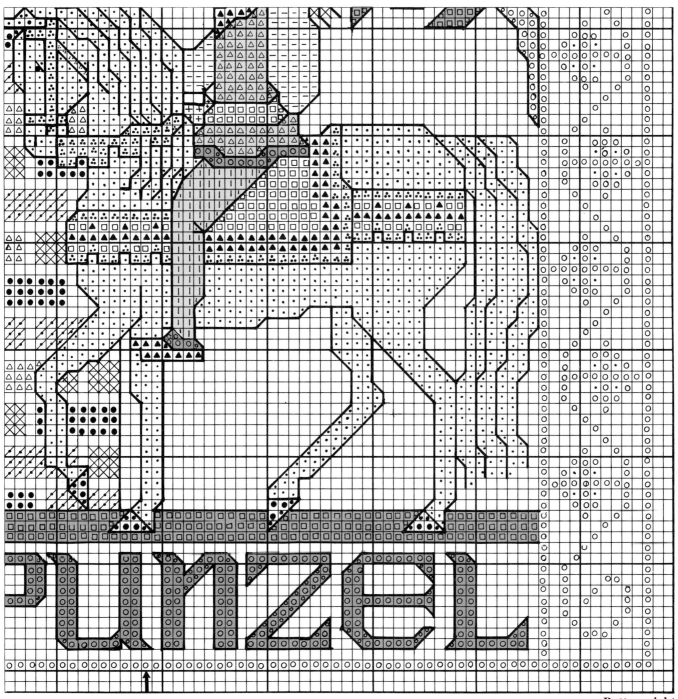

Bottom right

Rumplestiltskin

. . . The little man was certain the Queen could never guess his name, and the child would become his!

"Is your name Conrad?"

"No," he answered.

"Is it Harry?"

"It is not!" he cackled.

Then with a gleam in her eye, the Queen asked, "Would your name, perhaps, be Rumplestiltskin?"

Rumplestiltskin

Stitched on White Murano 30 over two threads, the finished design size is 5⅝" x 7⅜". The fabric was cut 17" x 17". As shown, pillow measures 20" x 20" including ruffle.

Other Fabrics	Finished Design
Aida 11	7¾" x 10¾"
Aida 14	6⅛" x 8⅜"
Aida 18	4¾" x 6½"
Hardanger 22	3⅞" x 5⅜"

The color key is found on page 56.

Pillow Materials

- 7¾ yards of 2½"–wide white eyelet
- Three white buttons (four holes)
- Three pink buttons (four holes)
- Green, white, and pink embroidery floss for buttons
- 1½ yards of 54"–wide pink print fabric
- 1 yard of ½"–wide lace trim
- 1½" yard of ½"–diameter cable cord for piping
- Matching thread
- #100/16 sewing machine needle
- Polyester stuffing

Large French knots: two strands, three wraps. Use pink floss for white buttons, white floss for pink buttons

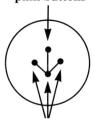

Long stitches with green floss: four strands

Button Diagram

Pillow Directions

All seams ½".

1. With completed design centered, cut piece 14" x 14". Cut 2½"–wide eyelet into four 14" strips. With right sides up and straight edges even, pin a length of eyelet to each edge of completed cross-stitch. Fold miters at corners, trim to ½" seam allowance and slip-stitch. Baste in place. Tack down points of eyelet.

2. From ½"–wide trim, cut two pieces 6⅝" long and two pieces 8⅜" long. Sew to completed cross-stitch, forming a lace border ½" beyond design border.

3. Referring to Button Diagram (left), sew buttons to sides of piece as shown in photo.

4. From pink print fabric, cut a 14" square and four 8" x 54" pieces; set aside. From remainder of fabric, make 1¼ yards of ½"–diameter corded piping; sew to pillow front (see General Instructions on bias strips and piping). Attach corded piping to perimeter of finished piece.

5. Sew all short ends of 8" x 54" pieces together to make a complete circle. Then press in half, wrong sides together and raw edges aligned. Cut four 54"-long pieces of 2½"–wide eyelet; sew together in same manner. Lay eyelet on top of fabric, straight edges aligned. Treating all three layers as one, gather each 54" section of the circle to 14". Pin to completed cross-stitch with right sides together, raw edges aligned, and seams at corners. Sew together.

6. Referring to General Instructions on finishing pillows, sew remaining 14" square to stitched piece. Turn right side out; stuff; slipstitch closed.

Top left • Stitch Count: 85 x 118

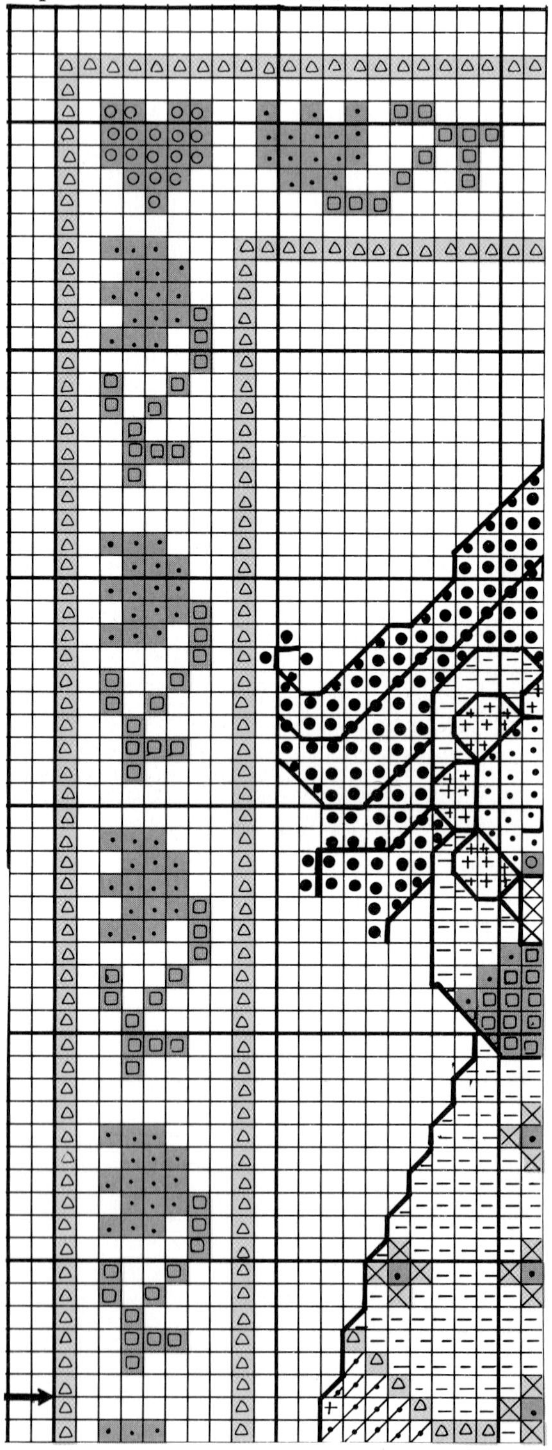

55

Rumplestiltskin

Anchor   **DMC (used for sample)**

Step 1: Cross-stitch (2 strands)

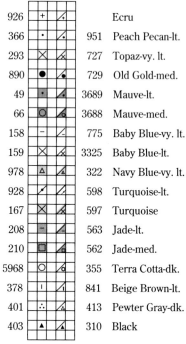

Anchor		DMC	
926	+ ⁄		Ecru
366	· ⁄	951	Peach Pecan-lt.
293	✕ ⧄	727	Topaz-vy. lt.
890	● ·	729	Old Gold-med.
49	·	3689	Mauve-lt.
66	⊙ ◹	3688	Mauve-med.
158	− ⁄	775	Baby Blue-vy. lt.
159	✕ ⧄	3325	Baby Blue-lt.
978	△ ◿	322	Navy Blue-vy. lt.
928	⁄ ⁄	598	Turquoise-lt.
167	✕ ⧄	597	Turquoise
208	− ⁄	563	Jade-lt.
210	▢ ⁄	562	Jade-med.
5968	⊙ ◹	355	Terra Cotta-dk.
378	¦ ⁄	841	Beige Brown-lt.
401	∴ ⧄	413	Pewter Gray-dk.
403	▲ ⁄	310	Black

Step 2: Backstitch (1 strand)

403	└─	310	Black

Step 3: French Knot (1 strand)

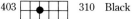

403	●	310	Black

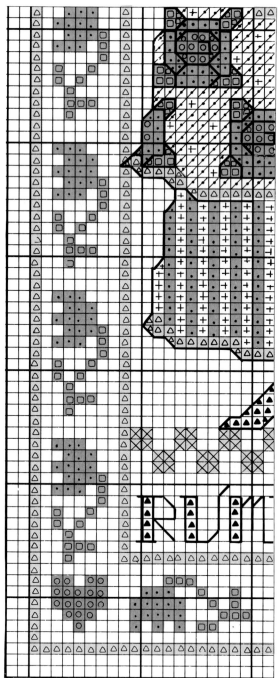

Bottom left

Nursery

The Old Woman who Lived in a Shoe

Ring A Ring O Roses

Rock-a-Bye Baby

Twinkle, Twinkle, Little Star

Rhymes

Little Bo Peep

Mary, Mary, Quite Contrary

Jack Sprat

Hey Diddle Diddle, the Cat and the Fiddle

Hey diddle, diddle,
    The cat and the fiddle,
The cow jumped
    Over the moon.

The little dog laughed,
    To see such a sport,
And the dish ran away
    With the spoon.

...The Cow Jumped
Over the Moon

Hey Diddle Diddle,
The Cat and the Fiddle . . .

SAMPLE
Stitched on Delicate Teal Jobelan 28 over two threads, the finished design size is 5⅝" x 8⅝". The fabric was cut 12" x 15". Frame as desired.

Other Fabrics	Finished Design
Aida 11	7⅛" x 10⅞"
Aida 14	5⅝" x 8⅝"
Aida 18	4⅜" x 6⅝"
Hardanger 22	3½" x 5½"

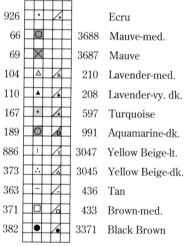

Anchor	DMC (used for sample)

Step 1: Cross-stitch (2 strands)

926			Ecru
66		3688	Mauve-med.
69		3687	Mauve
104		210	Lavender-med.
110		208	Lavender-vy. dk.
167		597	Turquoise
189		991	Aquamarine-dk.
886		3047	Yellow Beige-lt.
373		3045	Yellow Beige-dk.
363		436	Tan
371		433	Brown-med.
382		3371	Black Brown

Step 2: Backstitch (1 strand)

382		3371	Black Brown

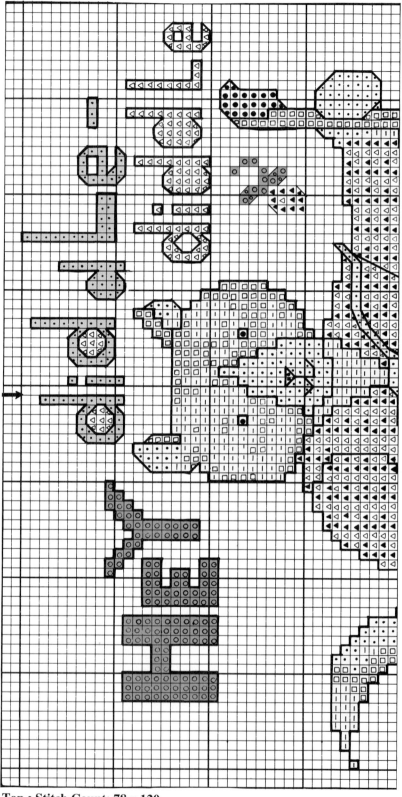

Top • Stitch Count: 78 x 120

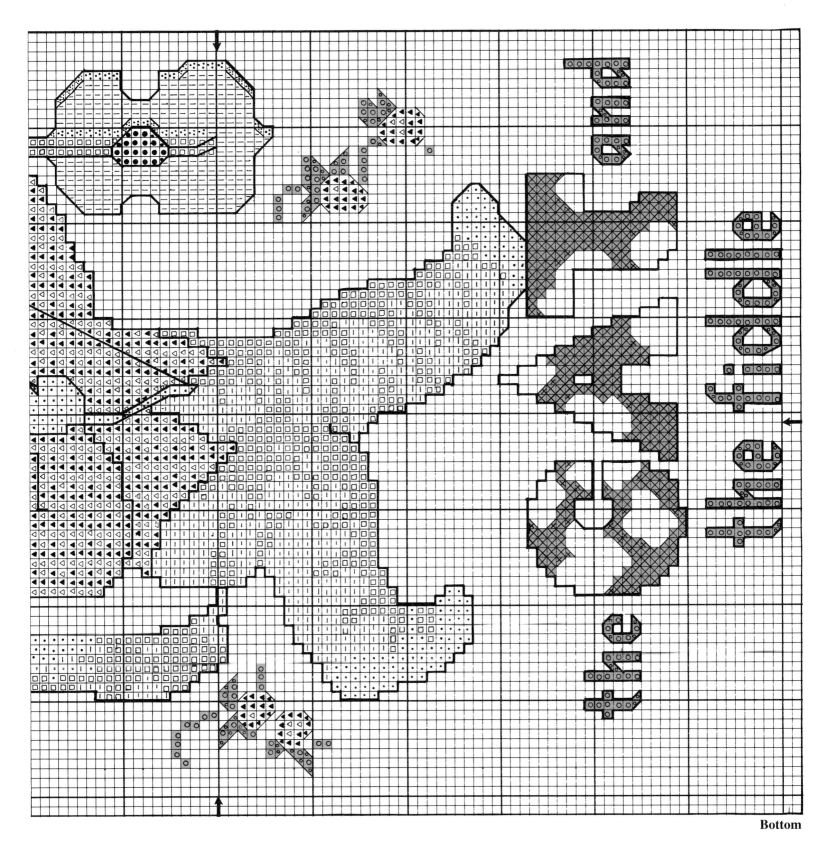

... The Cow Jumped Over the Moon

SAMPLE

Stitched on Ash Rose Murano 30 over two threads, the finished design size is 5⅛" x 8¾". The fabric was cut 12" x 15". Frame as desired.

Other Fabrics	Finished Design
Aida 11	6⅞" x 11⅞"
Aida 14	5½" x 9⅜"
Aida 18	4¼" x 7¼"
Hardanger 22	3½" x 6"

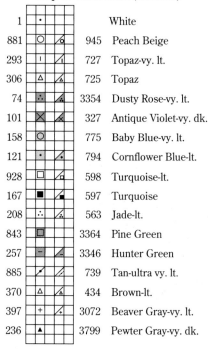

Anchor			DMC	(used for sample)

Step 1: Cross-stitch (2 strands)

1				White
881			945	Peach Beige
293			727	Topaz-vy. lt.
306			725	Topaz
74			3354	Dusty Rose-vy. lt.
101			327	Antique Violet-vy. dk.
158			775	Baby Blue-vy. lt.
121			794	Cornflower Blue-lt.
928			598	Turquoise-lt.
167			597	Turquoise
208			563	Jade-lt.
843			3364	Pine Green
257			3346	Hunter Green
885			739	Tan-ultra vy. lt.
370			434	Brown-lt.
397			3072	Beaver Gray-vy. lt.
236			3799	Pewter Gray-vy. dk.

Step 2: Backstitch (1 strand)

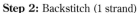

| 236 | | | 3799 | Pewter Gray-vy. dk. |

Step 3: French Knot (1 strand)

| 236 | | | 3799 | Pewter Gray-vy. dk. |

Top • Stitch Count: 76 x 131

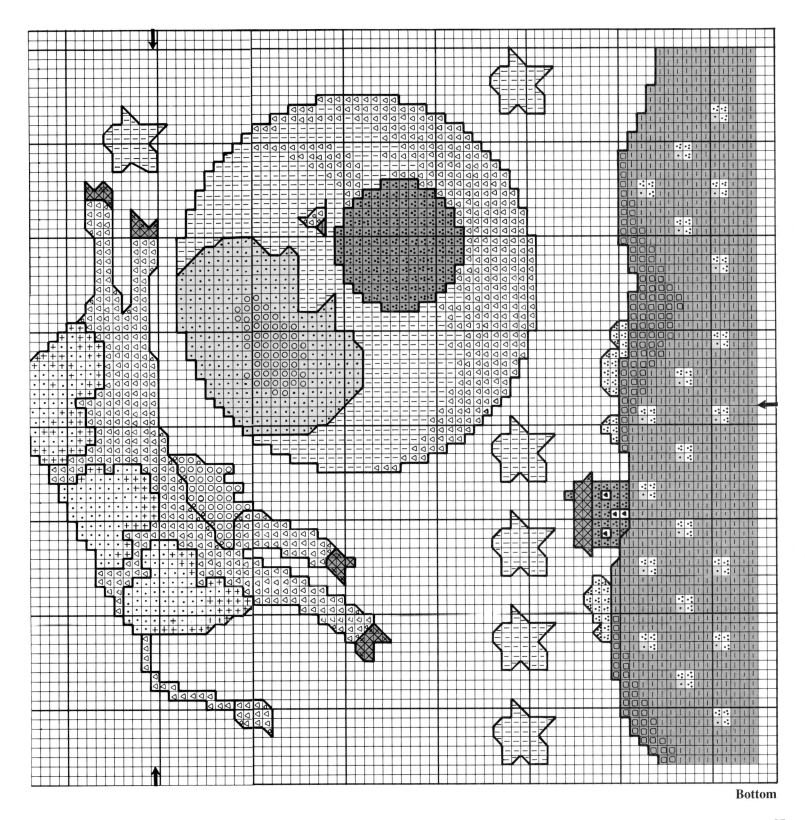

Bottom

Ring A Ring

Ring a ring o roses,
   A pocket full of posies.
Ashes, ashes,
   We all fall down!

O Roses

Ring A Ring O Roses

SAMPLE
Stitched on Light Mocha Belfast Linen 32 over two threads, the finished design size is 10" x 8½". The fabric was cut 16" x 15". Frame as desired.

Other Fabrics	Finished Design
Aida 11	14½" x 12⅜"
Aida 14	11⅜" x 9¾"
Aida 18	8⅞" x 7½"
Hardanger 22	7¼" x 6⅛"

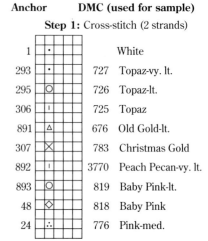

Anchor		DMC (used for sample)	
	Step 1: Cross-stitch (2 strands)		
1	·		White
293	·	727	Topaz-vy. lt.
295	O	726	Topaz-lt.
306	I	725	Topaz
891	△	676	Old Gold-lt.
307	✕	783	Christmas Gold
892	I	3770	Peach Pecan-vy. lt.
893	O	819	Baby Pink-lt.
48	◇	818	Baby Pink
24	∴	776	Pink-med.

Top left • Stitch Count: 160 x 136

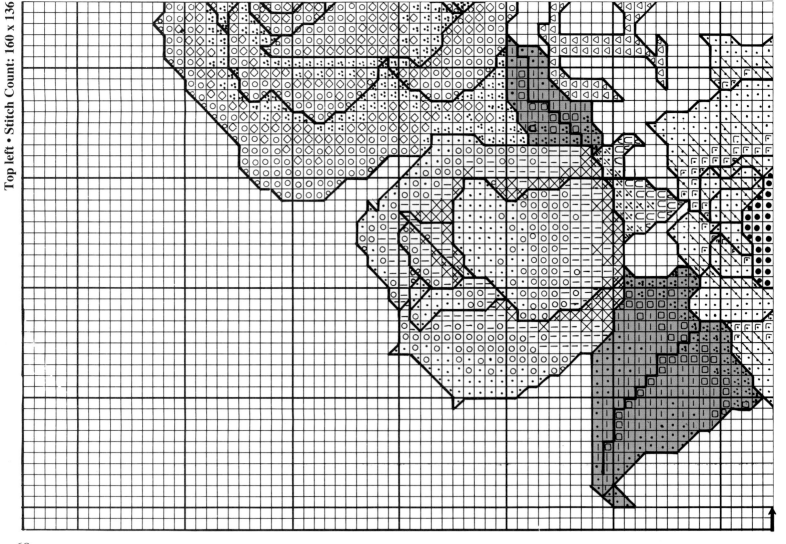

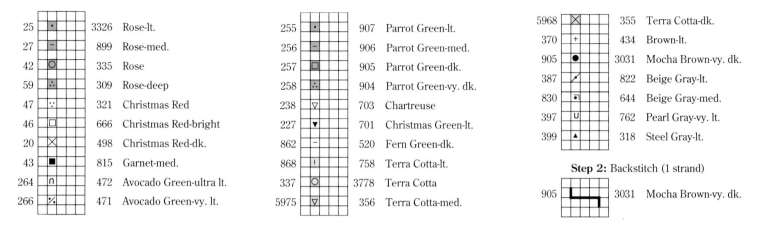

25		3326	Rose-lt.	255	907	Parrot Green-lt.
27		899	Rose-med.	256	906	Parrot Green-med.
42		335	Rose	257	905	Parrot Green-dk.
59		309	Rose-deep	258	904	Parrot Green-vy. dk.
47		321	Christmas Red	238	703	Chartreuse
46		666	Christmas Red-bright	227	701	Christmas Green-lt.
20		498	Christmas Red-dk.	862	520	Fern Green-dk.
43		815	Garnet-med.	868	758	Terra Cotta-lt.
264		472	Avocado Green-ultra lt.	337	3778	Terra Cotta
266		471	Avocado Green-vy. lt.	5975	356	Terra Cotta-med.

5968		355	Terra Cotta-dk.
370		434	Brown-lt.
905		3031	Mocha Brown-vy. dk.
387		822	Beige Gray-lt.
830		644	Beige Gray-med.
397		762	Pearl Gray-vy. lt.
399		318	Steel Gray-lt.

Step 2: Backstitch (1 strand)

905		3031	Mocha Brown-vy. dk.

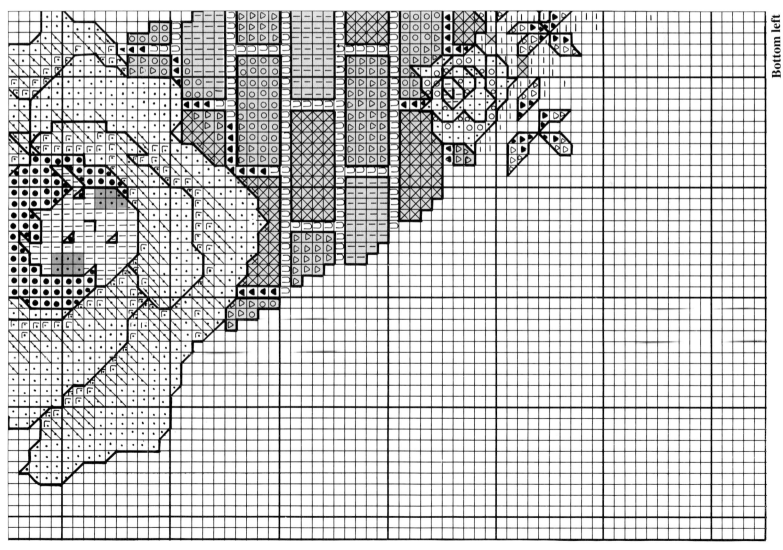

Bottom left

Ring A Ring O Roses

Top center

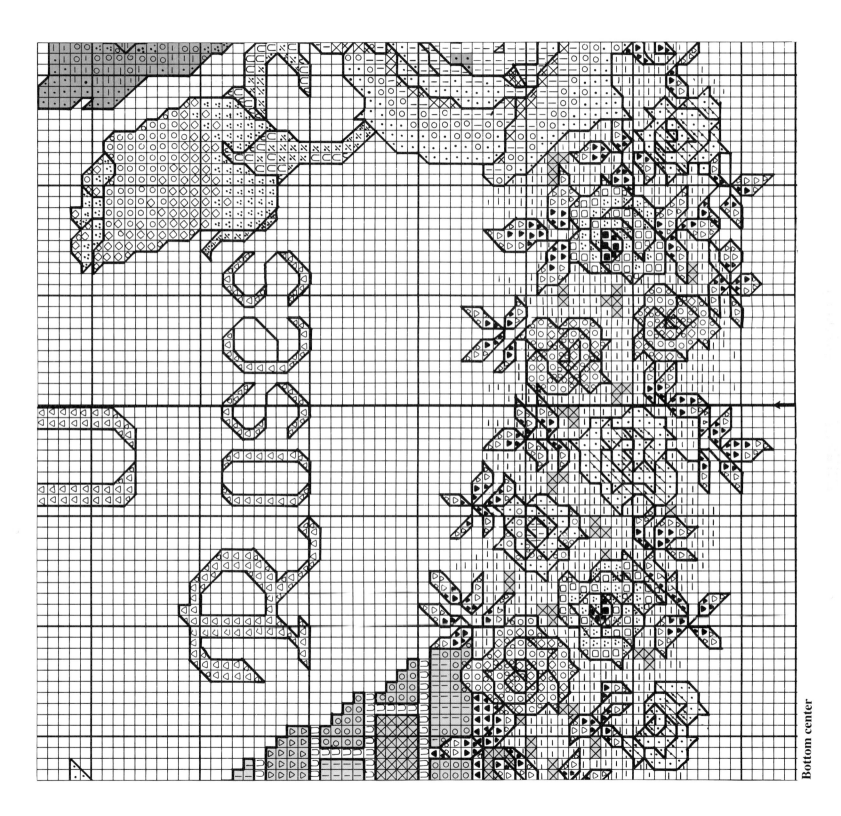

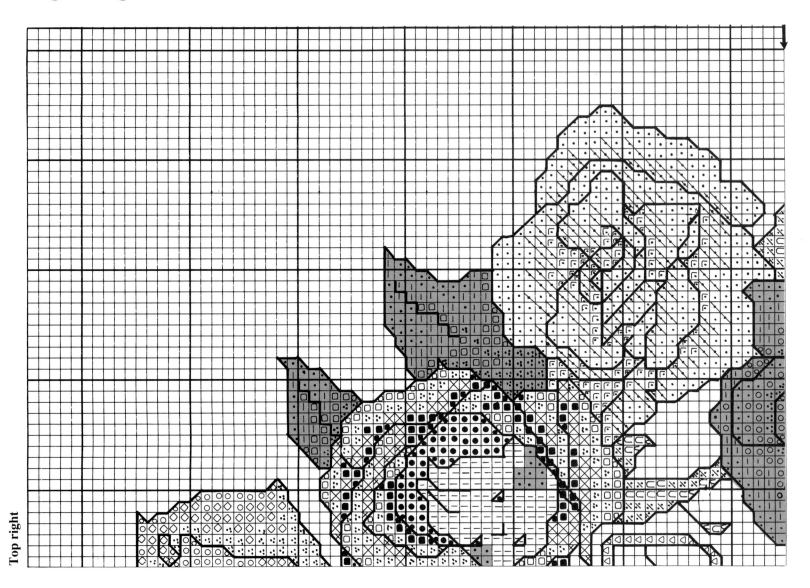

Top right

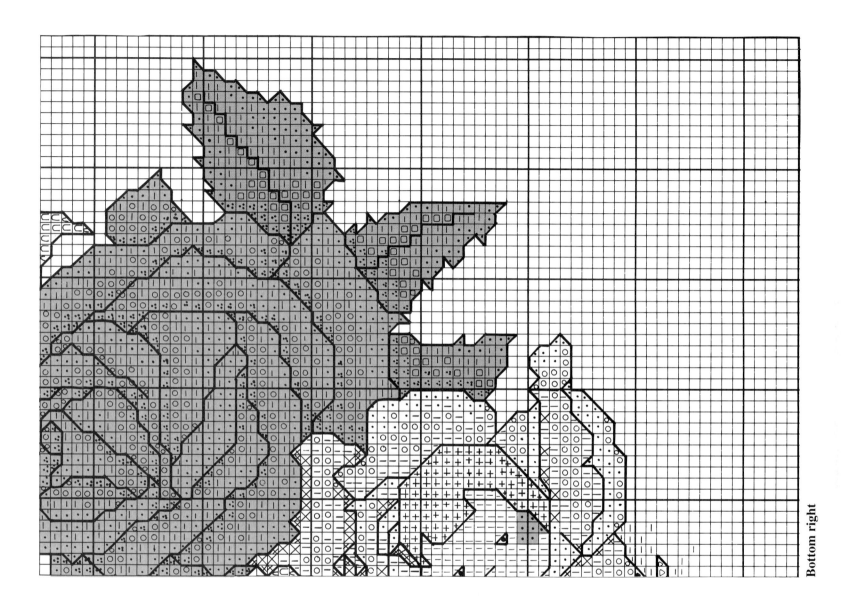

73

Rock-a-Bye Baby

Rock-a-bye baby
On the tree top,
When the wind blows
The cradle will rock.

When the bough breaks
The cradle will fall,
And down will come baby
Cradle and all.

Rock-a-Bye Baby

SAMPLE

Stitched on Cream Murano 30 over two threads, the finished design size is 7¾" x 10¼". The fabric was cut 14" x 17". Frame as desired.

Other Fabrics	Finished Design
Aida 11	10⅝" x 13⅞"
Aida 14	8⅜" x 10⅞"
Aida 18	6½" x 8½"
Hardanger 22	5⅜" x 7"

A child's name and birth date may be centered on a 14" x 6" piece of Cream Murano 30 over two threads, and framed below the cross-stitch piece. Use an alphabet found on pages 80 or 81.

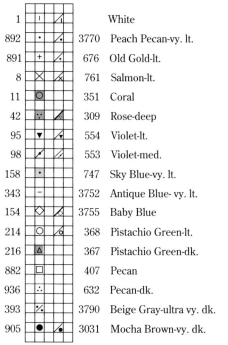

Anchor		DMC (used for sample)	

Step 1: Cross-stitch (2 strands)

1			White
892		3770	Peach Pecan-vy. lt.
891		676	Old Gold-lt.
8		761	Salmon-lt.
11		351	Coral
42		309	Rose-deep
95		554	Violet-lt.
98		553	Violet-med.
158		747	Sky Blue-vy. lt.
343		3752	Antique Blue- vy. lt.
154		3755	Baby Blue
214		368	Pistachio Green-lt.
216		367	Pistachio Green-dk.
882		407	Pecan
936		632	Pecan-dk.
393		3790	Beige Gray-ultra vy. dk.
905		3031	Mocha Brown-vy. dk.

Step 2: Backstitch (1 strand)

| 42 | | 309 | Rose-deep (Baby's mouth) |
| 905 | | 3031 | Mocha Brown-vy. dk. (All else) |

c

Top left • Stitch Count: 117 x 153

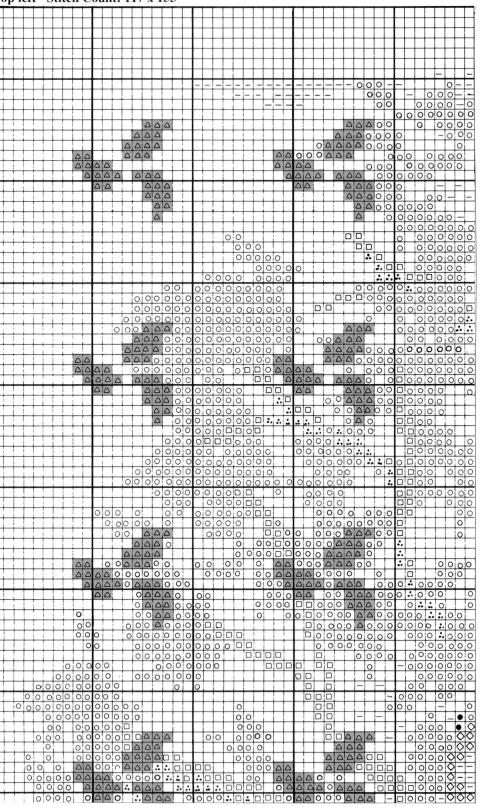

f

g

h

i

y

j

k

z

l

m

w

n

o

u

p

t

q

s

r

r

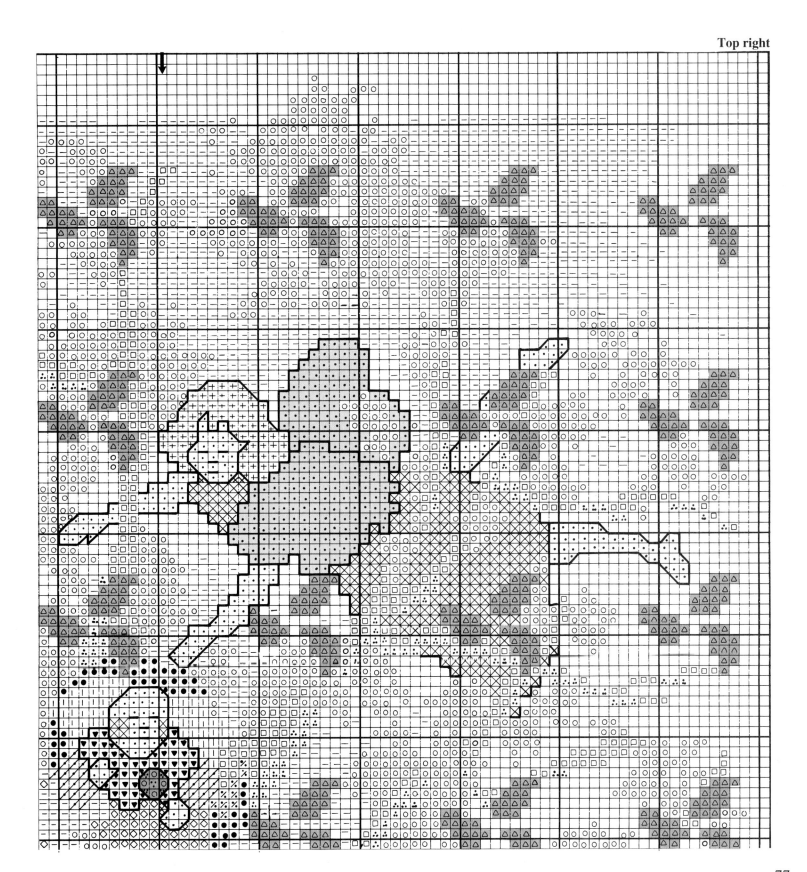

Rock-a-Bye Baby

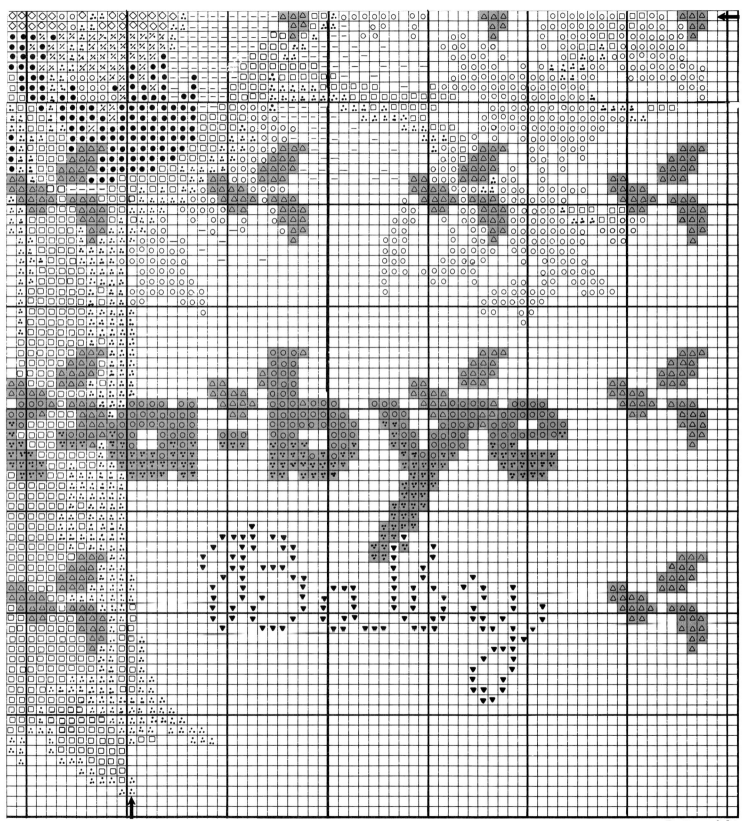

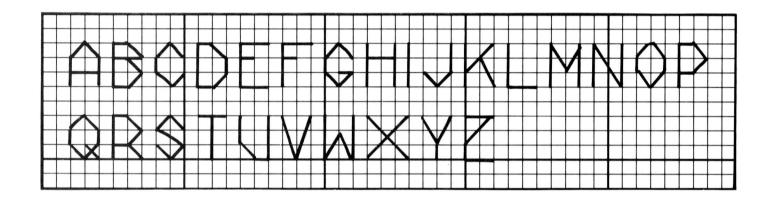

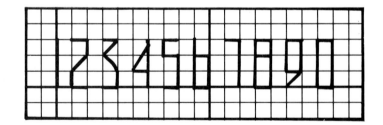

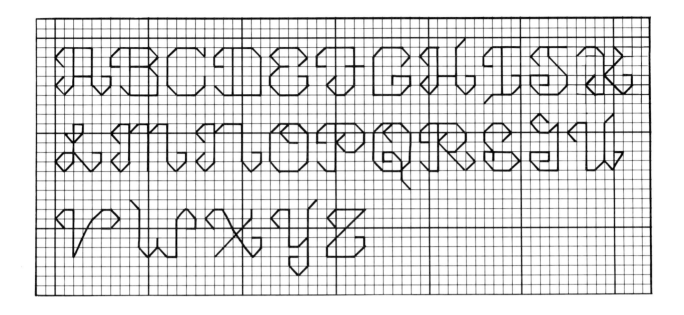

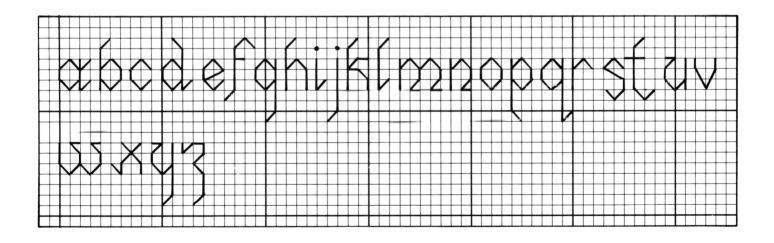

Jack Sprat
      Could eat no fat,
His wife
      Could eat no lean.
And so between
      The two of them,
They licked the
      Platter clean.

Jack Sprat

Jack Sprat

SAMPLE

Stitched on Antique White Belfast Linen 32 over two threads, the finished design size is 5⅛" x 5¾". The fabric was cut 12" x 12". Frame as desired.

Other Fabrics	Finished Design
Aida 11	7½" x 8¼"
Aida 14	5⅞" x 6½"
Aida 18	4½" x 5"
Hardanger 22	3¾" x 4⅛"

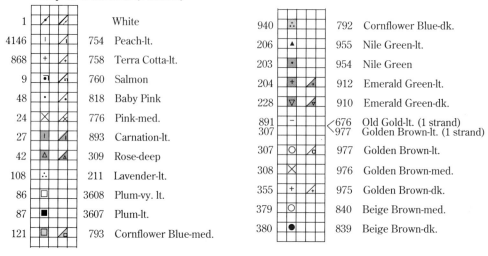

Anchor   **DMC (used for sample)**

Step 1: Cross-stitch (2 strands)

Anchor	DMC	Name
1	White	White
4146	754	Peach-lt.
868	758	Terra Cotta-lt.
9	760	Salmon
48	818	Baby Pink
24	776	Pink-med.
27	893	Carnation-lt.
42	309	Rose-deep
108	211	Lavender-lt.
86	3608	Plum-vy. lt.
87	3607	Plum-lt.
121	793	Cornflower Blue-med.
940	792	Cornflower Blue-dk.
206	955	Nile Green-lt.
203	954	Nile Green
204	912	Emerald Green-lt.
228	910	Emerald Green-dk.
891 / 307	676 / 977	Old Gold-lt. (1 strand) / Golden Brown-lt. (1 strand)
307	977	Golden Brown-lt.
308	976	Golden Brown-med.
355	975	Golden Brown-dk.
379	840	Beige Brown-med.
380	839	Beige Brown-dk.

Top left • Stitch Count: 82 x 91

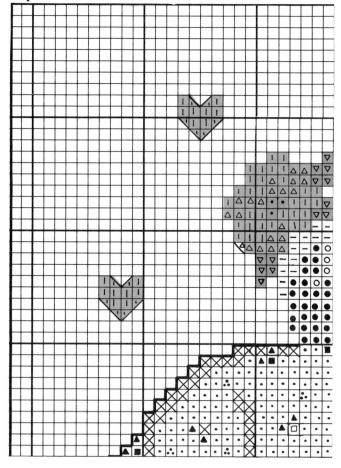

Step 2: Backstitch (1 strand)

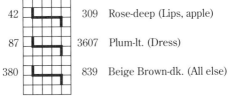

42		309	Rose-deep (Lips, apple)
87		3607	Plum-lt. (Dress)
380		839	Beige Brown-dk. (All else)

Step 3: French Knot (1 strand)

380   839   Beige Brown-dk.

Top right

Jack Sprat

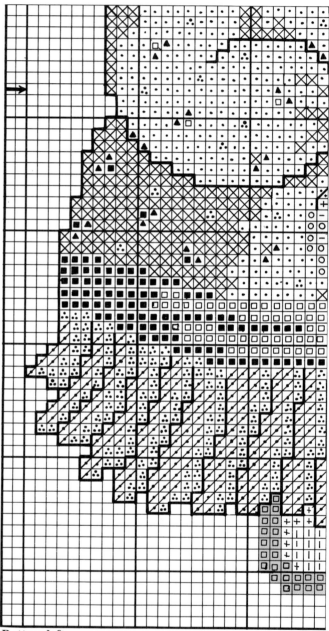

Bottom left

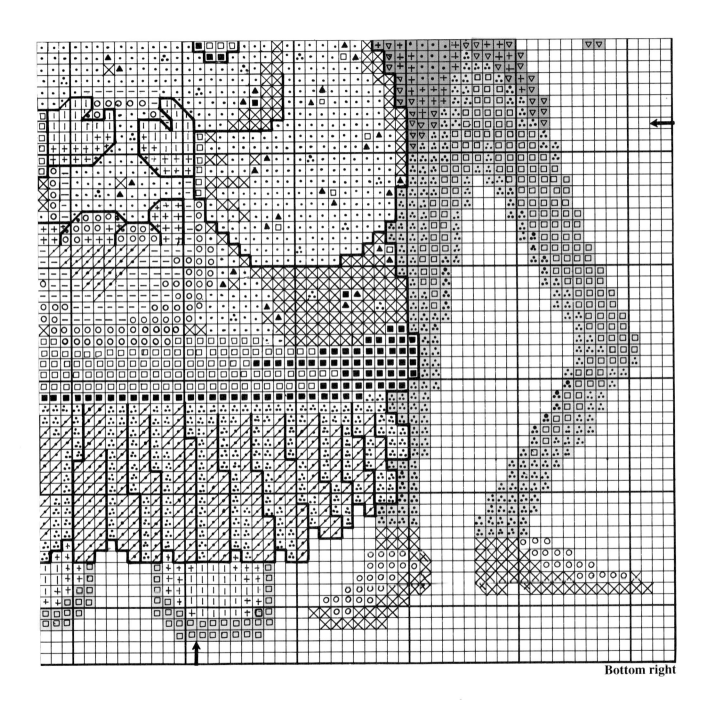

Bottom right

Little Bo Peep

Little Bo Peep
    Has lost her sheep
And doesn't know where
    To find them.

Leave them alone
    And they'll come home,
Wagging their tails
    Behind them.

Little Bo Peep

SAMPLE
Stitched on White Belfast Linen 32 over two threads, the finished design size is 7¾" x 7½". The fabric was cut 14" x 14".

Other Fabrics	Finished Design
Aida 11	11⅛" x 10⅞"
Aida 14	8¾" x 8½"
Aida 18	6⅞" x 6⅝"
Hardanger 22	5⅝" x 5⅜"

Clock Materials
- Sudbury House Clock without face
- 8-ounce bottle of light green acrylic paint
- 8-ounce bottle of dark walnut antiquing glaze
- Paper towels
- Purchased small wooden sheep and trees
- Gray, dark gray, brown, white, green, and yellow acrylic paints
- Small sponge
- Medium and small paintbrushes
- 6" piece of ⅜" pink satin ribbon
- 18" piece of ⅛" pink satin ribbon
- Pink thread
- hot-glue gun with glue sticks

Clock Directions

1. Paint clock with one coat of light green paint. Let dry. Dip brush in antiquing glaze. Remove excess glaze from brush and dab on a paper towel. Lightly brush piece so that the glaze streaks, but does not completely cover piece. Remove portions of wet glaze with towel or rag if needed.

2. Paint tree trunk brown and leaves green; sponge over leaves with white paint as desired. Paint sheep gray; sponge with white, except for feet and faces. Add details to face, ears, and legs with dark gray paint, referring to photo. Let dry. Tie 9" pieces of ⅛" pink satin ribbon around necks of sheep; trim as desired.

Top left • Stitch Count: 123 x 119

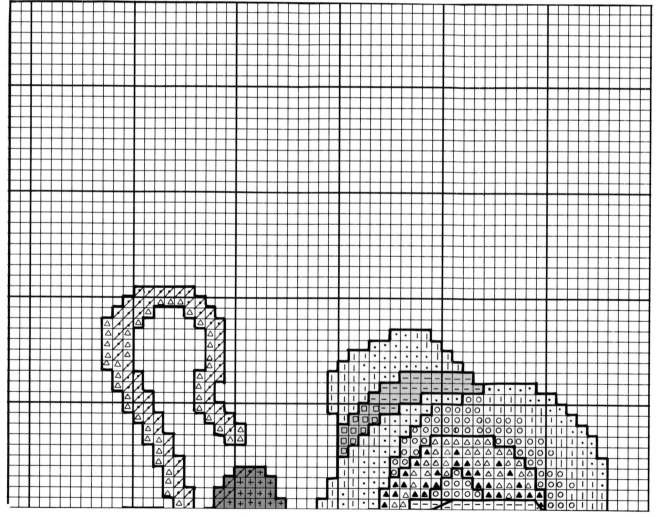

3. Tie ⅜" pink satin ribbon into a bow; sew onto staff as shown in photo.

4. Insert completed cross-stitch piece and assemble clock following manufacturer's instructions. Paint flowers on front of glass using green and yellow paints as shown. Hot-glue small wooden pieces to clock.

Anchor			DMC	(used for sample)
			Step 1: Cross-stitch (2 strands)	

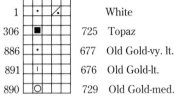

1	·	⁄		White
306	■		725	Topaz
886	·		677	Old Gold-vy. lt.
891	ı		676	Old Gold-lt.
890	O		729	Old Gold-med.

4146	–	⁄	754	Peach-lt.
868	O	⁄	758	Terra Cotta-lt.
24	+	⁄	776	Pink-med.
25	◪	⁄	3326	Rose-lt.
27	△	⁄	899	Rose-med.
76	∴	⁄	3731	Dusty Rose-med.
128	–		800	Delft-pale
130	□	⁄	809	Delft
121	✕	⁄	793	Cornflower Blue-med.
242	✕	⁄	989	Forest Green
338	⁄	⁄	3776	Mahogany-lt.
349	△	⁄	301	Mahogany-med.
352	▲	⁄	300	Mahogany-vy. dk.
397	□	⁄	762	Pearl Gray-vy. lt.
398	∴	⁄	415	Pearl Gray

Step 2: Long, loose stitch (2 strands)

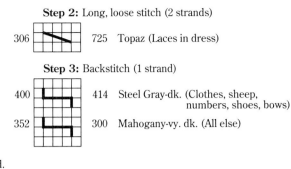

| 306 | | 725 | Topaz (Laces in dress) |

Step 3: Backstitch (1 strand)

| 400 | | 414 | Steel Gray-dk. (Clothes, sheep, numbers, shoes, bows) |
| 352 | | 300 | Mahogany-vy. dk. (All else) |

Top right

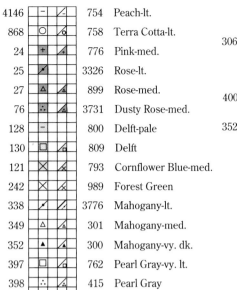

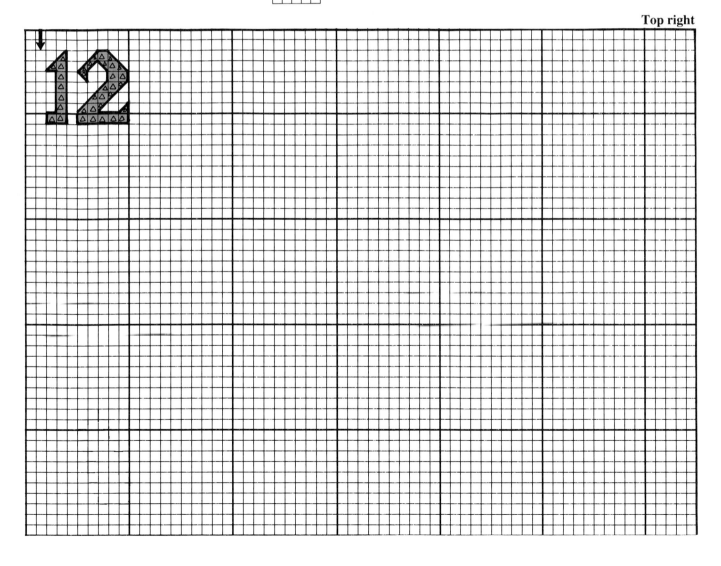

Little Bo Peep

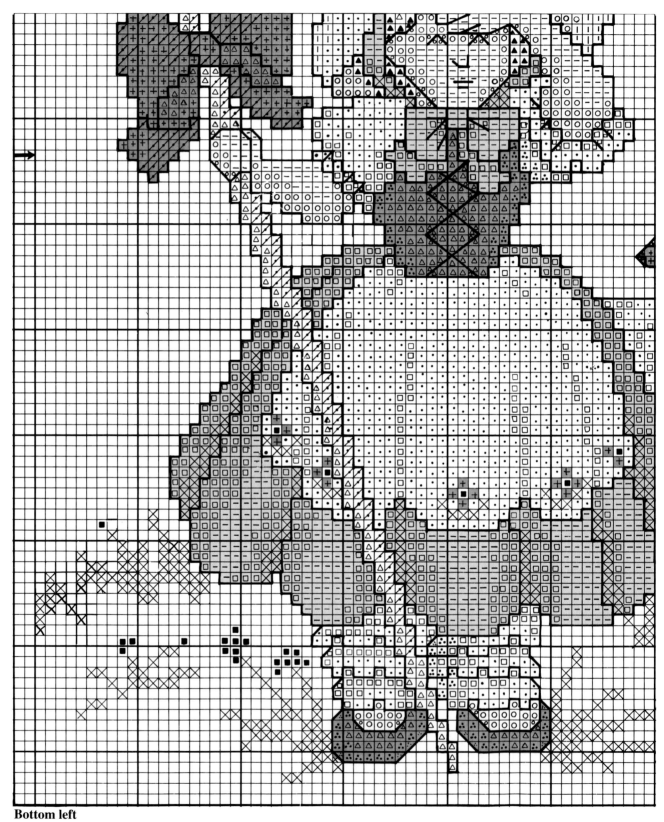

Bottom left

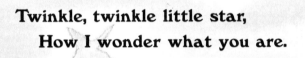

Twinkle, Twinkle Little Star

Twinkle, twinkle little star,
How I wonder what you are.

Up above the world so high,
Like a diamond in the sky!

Twinkle, Twinkle Little Star

SAMPLE

Stitched on Ivory Murano 30 over two threads, the finished design size is 6⅛" x 6⅜". The fabric was cut 13" x 13".

Other Fabrics	Finished Design
Aida 11	8⅜" x 8⅝"
Aida 14	6⅝" x 6¾"
Aida 18	5⅛" x 5¼"
Hardanger 22	4⅛" x 4⅜"

The color key is found on page 98.

Box Materials

- Box with 6½" x 6½" insert (See suppliers, page 167)
- Small sponge
- Purple, blue, pink, and yellow acrylic paints
- 3" x 5" index card
- Small paintbrush
- Foamcore or heavy cardboard same size as opening on box top
- Straight pins, or hot-glue gun and glue sticks
- Small pieces of polyester batting
- Newspaper or paper towel

Box Directions

1. Dab a small sponge in purple, blue, or pink paint and blot excess paint onto newspaper or paper towel. When desired effect is achieved on paper, dab paint onto box. Repeat with remaining colors until entire box is covered with a pleasing blend. Allow to dry completely.

2. Cut a star stencil from index card. Randomly sponge-paint yellow stars through the stencil onto sides of box (or paint them freehand with a small paintbrush).

3. Cut board to fit box top opening. Layer and hot-glue polyester batting on top of board to desired thickness. Pin or hot-glue completed cross-stitch piece to underside of Foamcore or cardboard. Insert into box.

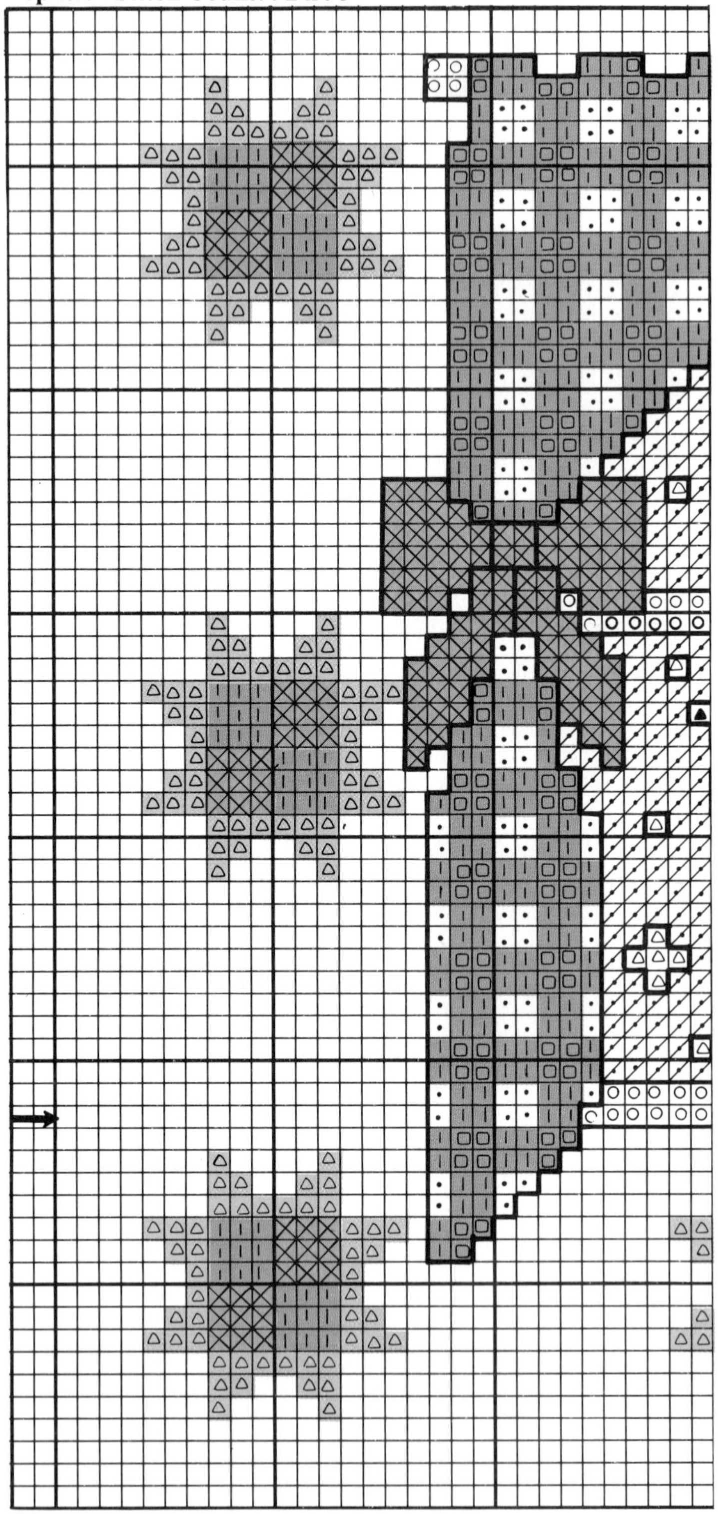

Twinkle, Twinkle Little Star

Anchor   DMC (used for sample)

Step 1: Cross-stitch (2 strands)

1		White
293	727	Topaz-vy. lt.
306	725	Topaz
891	676	Old Gold-lt.
890	729	Old Gold-med.
892	225	Shell Pink-vy. lt.
75	3733	Dusty Rose-lt.
118	340	Blue Violet-med.
922	930	Antique Blue-dk.
185	964	Seagreen-lt.
187	992	Aquamarine
206	955	Nile Green-lt.
899	3782	Mocha Brown-lt.
400	414	Steel Gray-dk.
236	3799	Pewter Gray-vy. dk.

Step 2: Backstitch (1 strand)

| 236 | 3799 | Pewter Gray-vy. dk. |

Step 3: French Knot (1 strand)

| 236 | 3799 | Pewter Gray-vy. dk. |

Bottom left

98

Twinkle little Star

Mary,

Mary,

Quite

Contrary

Mary, Mary, quite contrary
How does your garden grow?

With silver bells and cockle shells
And pretty maids all in a row?

Mary, Mary, Quite Contrary

SAMPLE
Stitched on Cream Murano 30 over two
threads, the finished design size is
6¼" x 10½". The fabric was cut 13" x 17".
Frame as desired.

Other Fabrics	Finished Design
Aida 11	8½" x 14⅜"
Aida 14	6⅝" x 11¼"
Aida 18	5⅛" x 8¾"
Hardanger 22	4¼" x 7⅛"

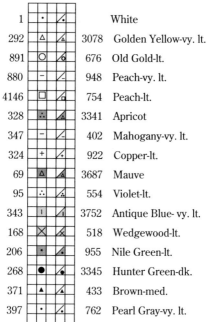

Anchor   DMC (used for sample)

Step 1: Cross-stitch (2 strands)

Anchor			DMC	
1	·	⁄		White
292	△	⁄	3078	Golden Yellow-vy. lt.
891	O	⁄	676	Old Gold-lt.
880	−	⁄	948	Peach-vy. lt.
4146	□	⁄	754	Peach-lt.
328	▪	⁄	3341	Apricot
347	−	⁄	402	Mahogany-vy. lt.
324	+	⁄	922	Copper-lt.
69	△	⁄	3687	Mauve
95	∴	⁄	554	Violet-lt.
343	I	⁄	3752	Antique Blue- vy. lt.
168	✕	⁄	518	Wedgewood-lt.
206	▪	⁄	955	Nile Green-lt.
268	●	⁄	3345	Hunter Green-dk.
371	▲	⁄	433	Brown-med.
397	·	⁄	762	Pearl Gray-vy. lt.

Step 2: Backstitch (1 strand)

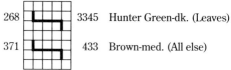

268		3345	Hunter Green-dk. (Leaves)
371		433	Brown-med. (All else)

Step 3: French Knot (1 strand)

371	●	433	Brown-med.

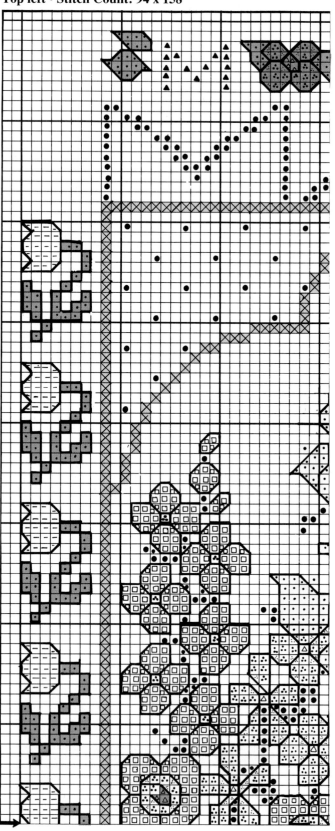

103

Mary, Mary, Quite Contrary

Bottom left

Contrary--How
our garden grow?

The Old Woman

Steven
Cass
Andrew
Katie
Cole
Lisa
Sara

Who Lived in a Shoe

There was an old woman,
Who lived in a shoe.

She had so many children,
She didn't know what to do . . .

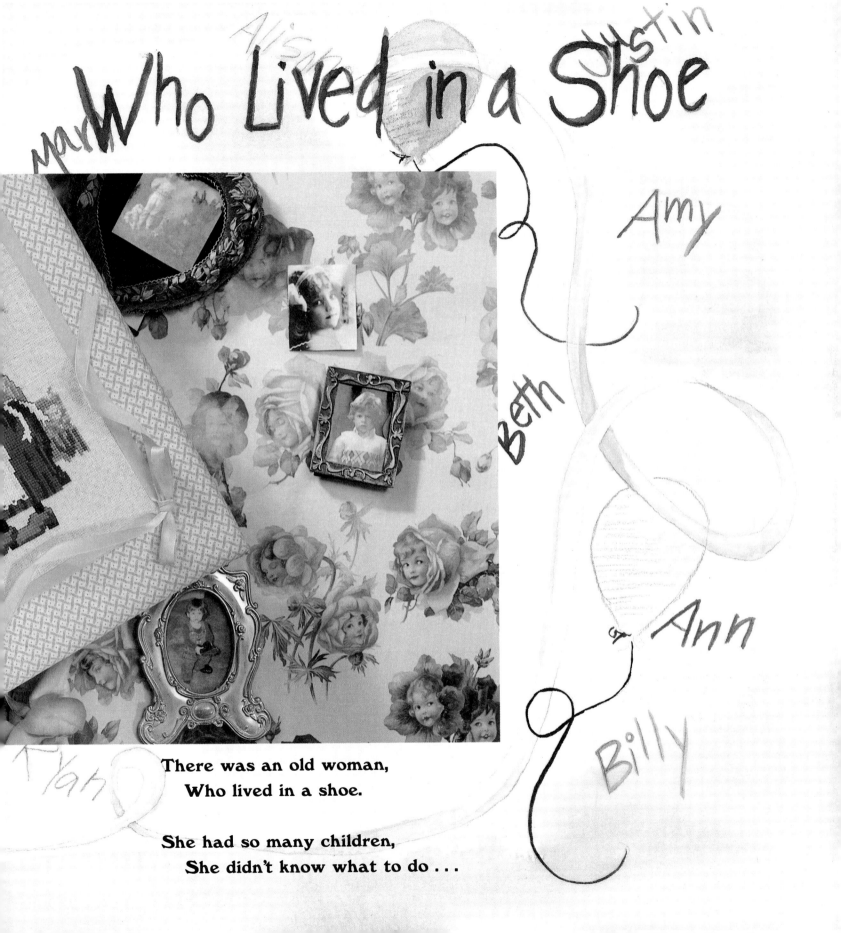

The Old Woman Who Lived in a Shoe

SAMPLE
Stitched on Cream Belfast Linen 32 over two threads, the finished design size is 9¼" x 7½". The fabric was cut 16" x 14".

Other Fabrics	Finished Design
Aida 11	13⅜" x 10⅞"
Aida 14	10½" x 8⅝"
Aida 18	8⅛" x 6⅝"
Hardanger 22	6⅝" x 5½"

Photo Album Materials

- Fabric-covered photo album
- Paper-backed fusible web
- ⅜"–wide ribbon: 1 yard, or enough to trim completed cross-stitch, including bow
- Fabric glue

Photo Album Directions

1. Cut fusible interfacing and completed cross-stitch piece to desired size (same size). Following manufacturer's instructions, fuse interfacing to wrong side of finished piece, then center and fuse piece to photo album.

2. Place midpoint of ribbon on upper left corner of cross-stitch. Fold ribbon to miter corner (see photo) and secure with glue. Continue gluing ribbon to perimeter of cross-stitch, mitering the corners, until ribbon meets in lower right corner. Tie ribbon in bow, and secure middle knot and ends of bow to album with glue.

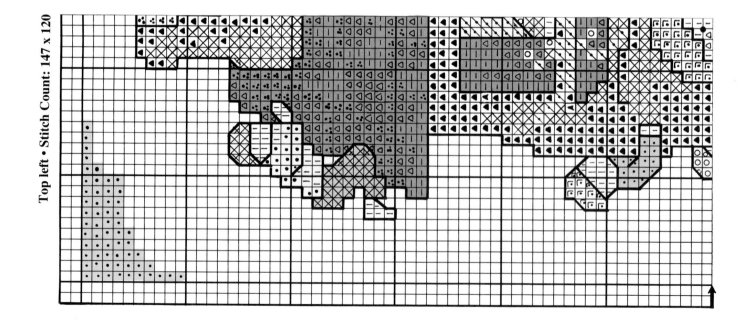

Top left • Stitch Count: 147 x 120

Anchor **DMC (used for sample)**

Step 1: Cross-stitch (2 strands)

Anchor			DMC	Name
1	·	⁄		White
301	⁄	⁄	744	Yellow-pale
891	▫	⁄	676	Old Gold-lt.
4146			⁄	754	Peach-lt.
9	△	⁄	760	Salmon
24	+	⁄	776	Pink-med.
26	○	⁄	957	Geranium-pale
76	●	⁄	961	Wild Rose-dk.
11	−	⁄	350	Coral-med.
13	△	⁄	349	Coral-dk.
22	∴	⁄	816	Garnet
99	▫	⁄	552	Violet-dk.
101	■	⁄	550	Violet-vy. dk.
128	·		800	Delft-pale
130	▫	⁄	799	Delft-med.
132	✕	⁄	797	Royal Blue

Anchor			DMC	Name
264	·	⁄	772	Pine Green-lt.
242	⁄	⁄	989	Forest Green
246	∴	⁄	986	Forest Green-vy. dk.
338	∵	⁄	3776	Mahogany-lt.
349	✕	⁄	301	Mahogany-med.
352	▲	⁄	300	Mahogany-vy. dk.
360	✕	⁄	898	Coffee Brown-vy. dk.
382	○	⁄	3371	Black Brown
397	I	⁄	762	Pearl Gray-vy. lt.

Step 2: Backstitch (1 strand)

			DMC	Name
338			3776	Mahogany-lt. (Daisies)
382			3371	Black Brown (All else)

Step 3: French Knot (1 strand)

			DMC	Name
382	●		3371	Black Brown

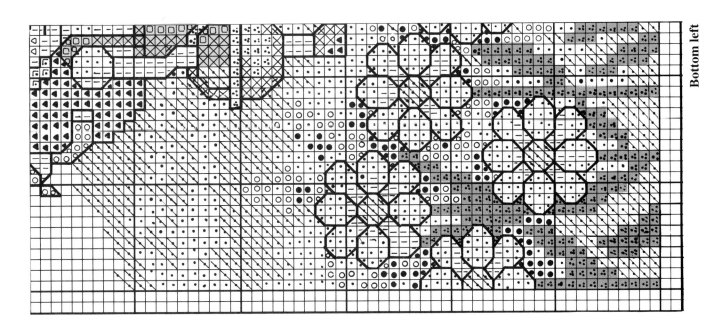

Bottom left

109

The Old Woman Who Lived in a Shoe

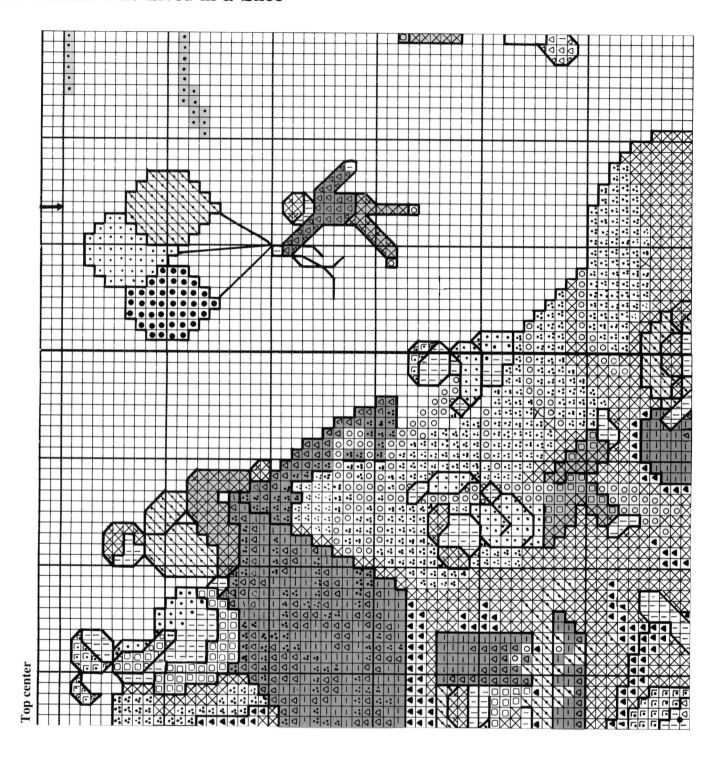

Top center

110

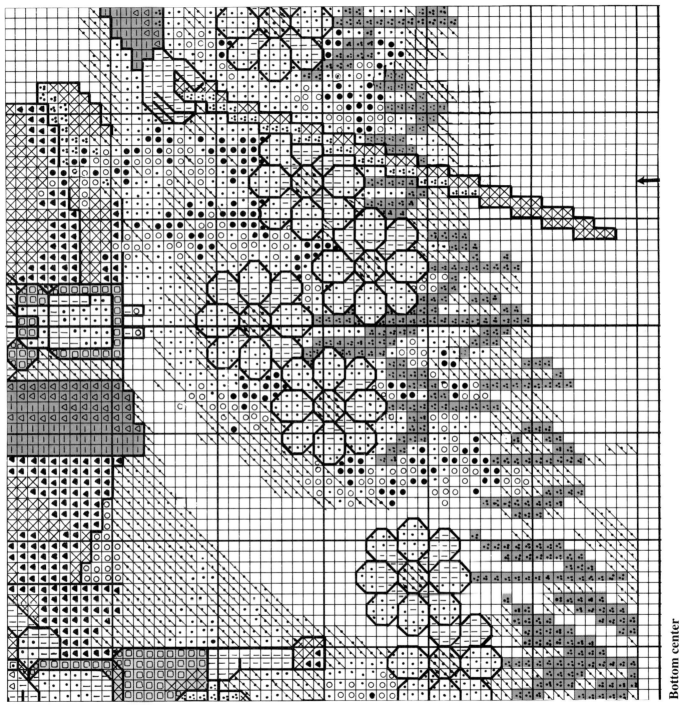

111

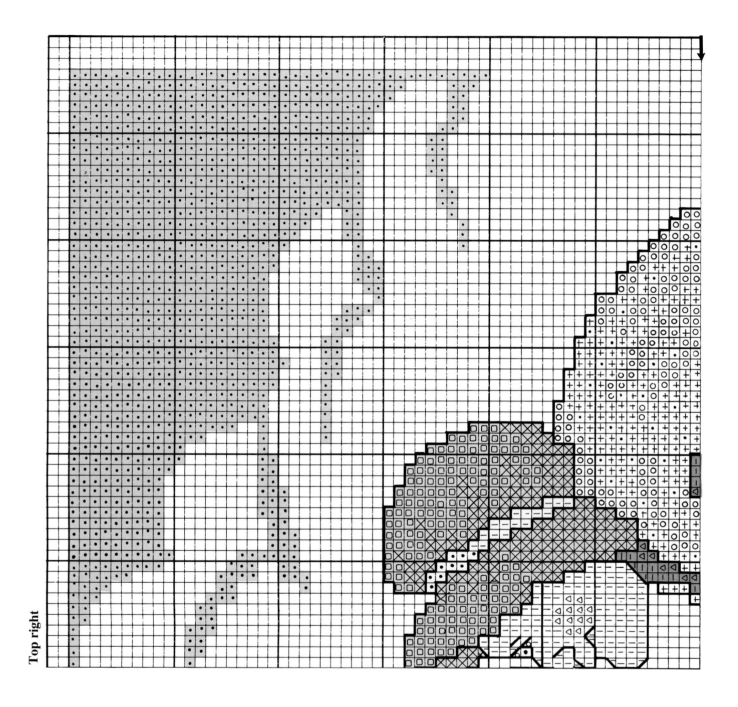

The Old Woman Who Lived in a Shoe

Top right

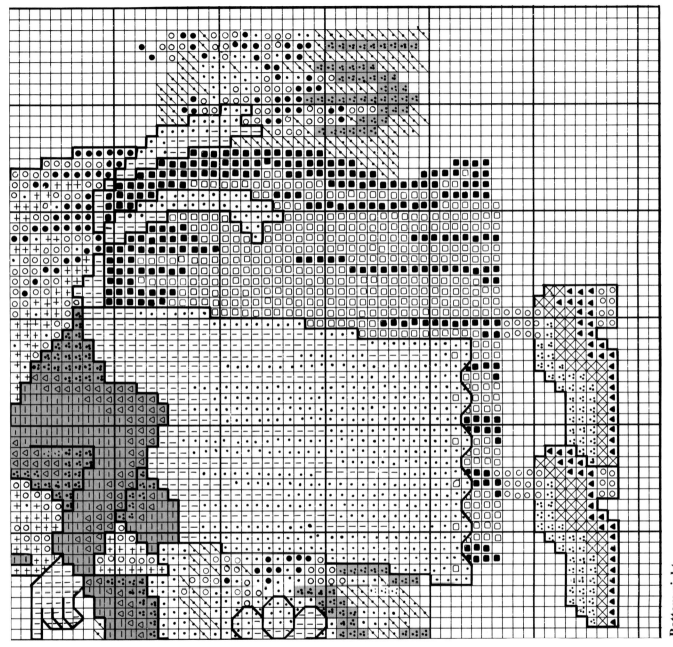

Fables

The Leopard and the Fox

The Wind and the Sun

The Wolf in Sheep's Clothing

Androcles and the Lion

The Goose that Laid the Golden Egg

The Tortoise and the Hare

The Fisherman and His Wife

The Country mouse and City m

The Goose
that laid the
golden egg

The Goose that Laid

Once there was an old man who owned a special goose that could lay golden eggs. Every day he would take her one egg into town and exchange it for money. One day he said to himself, "This goose must be full of eggs. If I could get them all at once, I would have much more money." So the man killed the goose, but when he cut her open, there were no golden eggs inside. As a reward for his impatience and greed, he lost everything he had.

the Golden Egg

The Goose that Laid the Golden Egg

SAMPLE

Stitched on Sand Belfast Linen 32 over two threads, the finished design size is 5⅛" x 8½". The fabric was cut 15" x 19". As shown, pillow measures 11¼" x 15".

Other Fabrics	Finished Design
Aida 11	7½" x 12½"
Aida 14	5⅞" x 9¾"
Aida 18	4½" x 7⅝"
Hardanger 22	3¾" x 6¼"

Pillow Materials

- ½ yard of 45" paisley fabric
- 1⅝ yard of ½"-diameter green braided satin piping for edge
- 1⅛ yard of ⅛"-diameter gold piping
- Paper-backed fusible web
- Matching thread
- Polyester stuffing

Pillow Directions

All seams are ½".

1. From print fabric, cut two pieces 12" x 3" and two pieces 16" x 3". Sew pieces together to form a rectangular fabric frame, mitering the corners.

2. Referring to General Instructions on piping, sew gold piping to the inner edges of the fabric frame.

3. Cut four pieces of fusible web to same dimensions as fabric for Step 1. Following manufacturer's instructions, fuse to the wrong side of the frame. Remove paper; center and fuse frame to stitched piece. Trim edges even. Sew braided piping to perimeter.

4. Cut 12½" x 16½" rectangle from paisley fabric for backing. Referring to General Instructions on finishing pillows, sew back to front, turn right side out and stuff. Slipstitch closed.

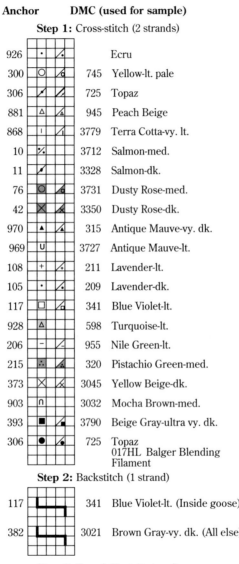

Anchor **DMC (used for sample)**

Step 1: Cross-stitch (2 strands)

Anchor	DMC	Color
926		Ecru
300	745	Yellow-lt. pale
306	725	Topaz
881	945	Peach Beige
868	3779	Terra Cotta-vy. lt.
10	3712	Salmon-med.
11	3328	Salmon-dk.
76	3731	Dusty Rose-med.
42	3350	Dusty Rose-dk.
970	315	Antique Mauve-vy. dk.
969	3727	Antique Mauve-lt.
108	211	Lavender-lt.
105	209	Lavender-dk.
117	341	Blue Violet-lt.
928	598	Turquoise-lt.
206	955	Nile Green-lt.
215	320	Pistachio Green-med.
373	3045	Yellow Beige-dk.
903	3032	Mocha Brown-med.
393	3790	Beige Gray-ultra vy. dk.
306	725	Topaz 017HL Balger Blending Filament

Step 2: Backstitch (1 strand)

Anchor	DMC	Color
117	341	Blue Violet-lt. (Inside goose)
382	3021	Brown Gray-vy. dk. (All else)

Step 3: French Knot (1 strand)

Anchor	DMC	Color
382	3021	Brown Gray-vy. dk.

Top left • Stitch Count: 82 x 137

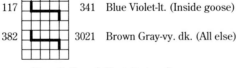

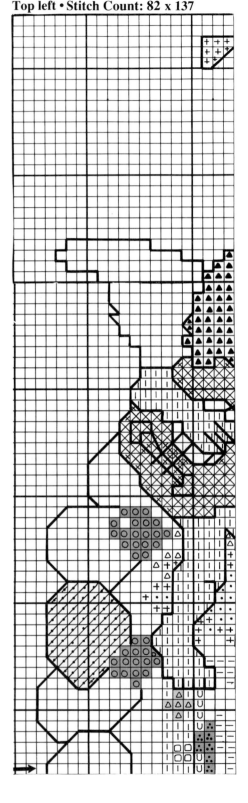

119

The Goose that Laid the Golden Egg

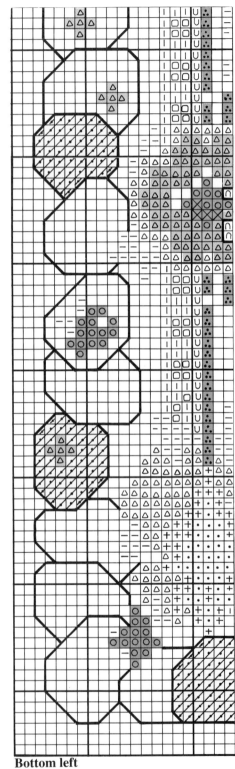

Bottom left

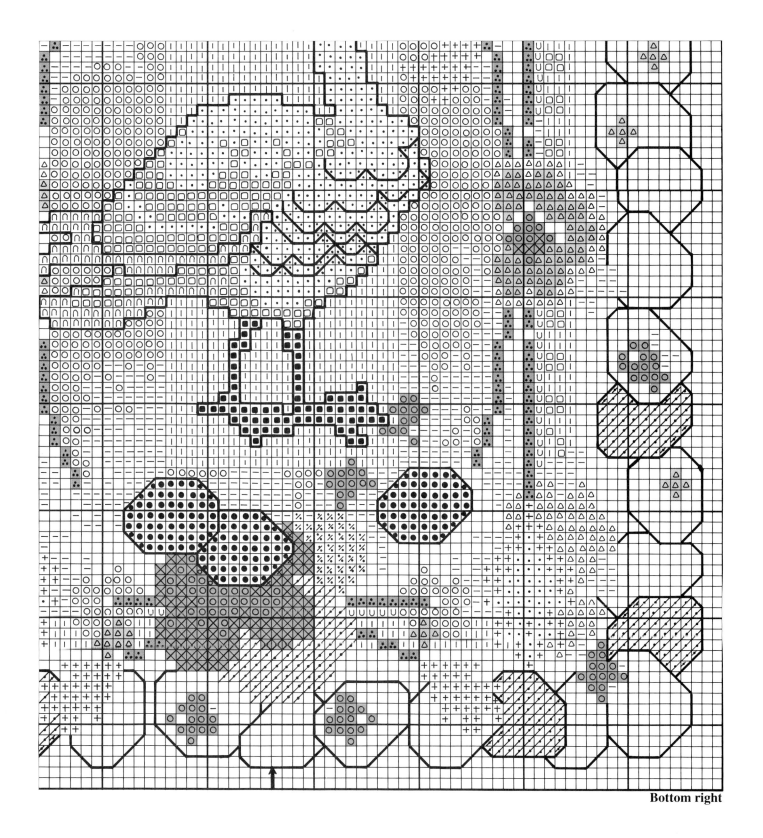

The Wind and the Sun were arguing about which was the stronger when they saw a man walking down the road. The sun said, "Whichever one of us can cause that traveler to take off his coat is the stronger."

The Sun went behind a cloud as the Wind blew hard upon the man. The man felt the cold and held the coat tightly around his shoulders. Then the Sun came out and shone brightly. The man found the sunshine delightful, and removed his cloak to enjoy it.

"Warmth and persuasion are always more powerful than cold force," said the Sun.

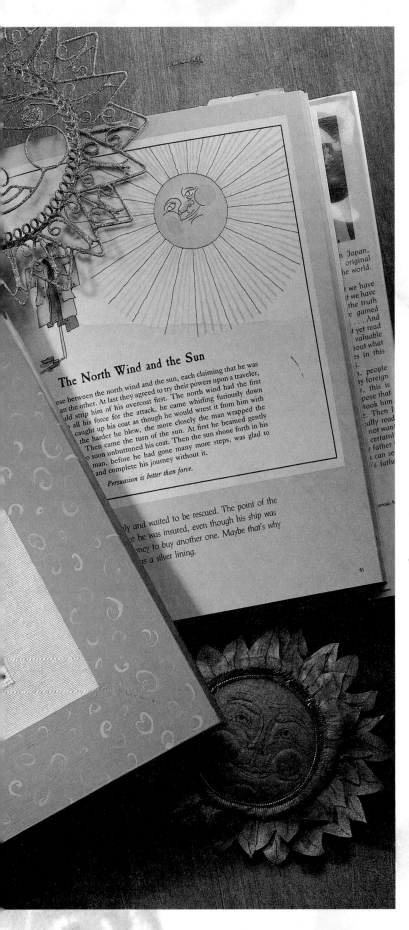

The Wind and the Sun

The Wind and the Sun

SAMPLE

Stitched on Platinum Belfast Linen 32 over two threads, the finished design size is 6¾" x 9". The fabric was cut 13" x 15". Frame as desired.

Other Fabrics	Finished Design
Aida 11	9⅞" x 13"
Aida 14	7¾" x 10¼"
Aida 18	6" x 8"
Hardanger 22	5" x 6½"

Anchor			DMC	(used for sample)

Step 1: Cross-stitch (2 strands)

892	3770	Peach Pecan-vy. lt.
891	676	Old Gold-lt.
337	3778	Terra Cotta
870	3042	Antique Violet-lt.
872	3740	Antique Violet-dk.
928	598	Turquoise-lt.
920	932	Antique Blue-lt.
921	931	Antique Blue-med.
900	928	Slate Green-lt.
905	3781	Mocha Brown-dk.
236	3799	Pewter Gray-vy. dk.

Step 2: Backstitch (1 strand)

236	3799	Pewter Gray-vy. dk.

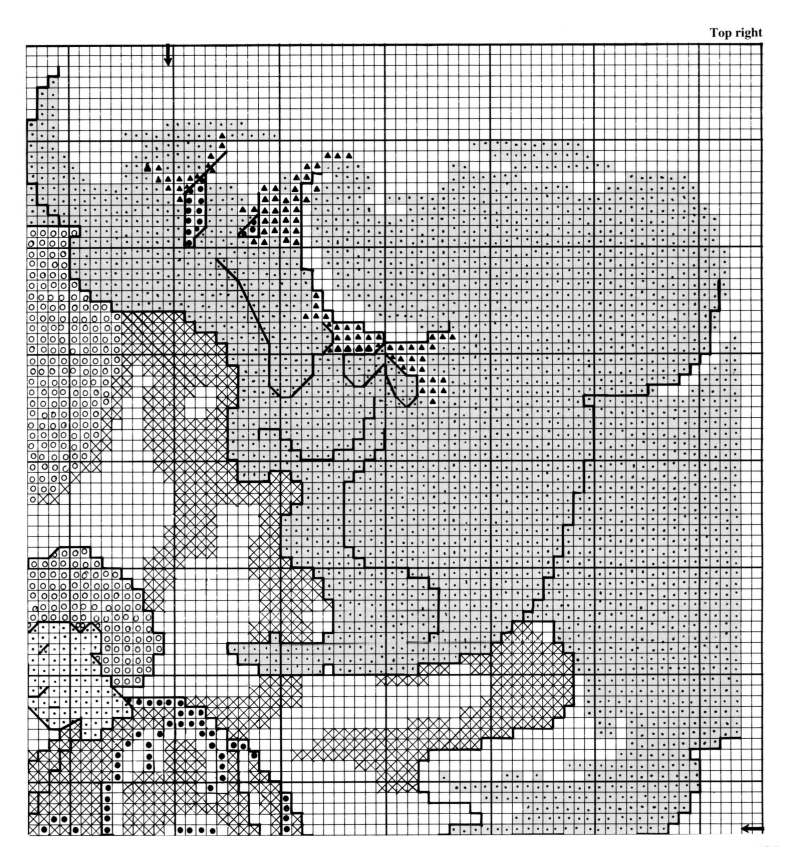

The Wind and the Sun

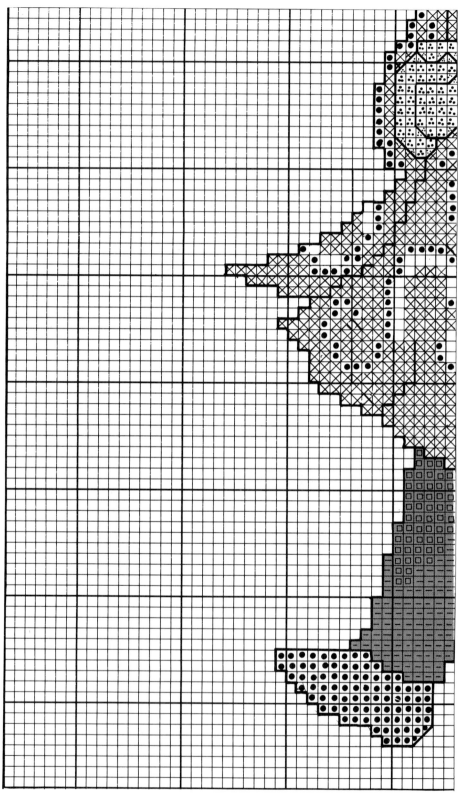

Bottom left

A Wolf in Sheep's Clothing

Once there was an old wolf who liked to eat sheep. Day after day he watched them, but he could not catch any because of the diligent shepherd. One day he found a sheep's skin. He put it on his back and went to graze with the sheep. They were not afraid of him because he looked like them. He crept up beside a fat lamb and quickly gobbled him up.

"So beware of a wolf who is all white and woolish. He's liable to eat a lamb that is foolish!"

A Wolf in Sheep's Clothing

SAMPLE

Stitched on Amaretto Murano 30
over two threads, the finished design size is
$4\frac{7}{8}$" x $7\frac{1}{8}$". The fabric was cut 11" x 13".
Frame as desired.

Other Fabrics	Finished Design
Aida 11	$7\frac{1}{8}$" x $10\frac{3}{8}$"
Aida 14	$5\frac{5}{8}$" x $8\frac{1}{8}$"
Aida 18	$4\frac{3}{8}$" x $6\frac{3}{8}$"
Hardanger 22	$3\frac{1}{2}$" x $5\frac{1}{8}$"

Anchor   **DMC (used for sample)**

Step 1: Cross-stitch (2 strands)

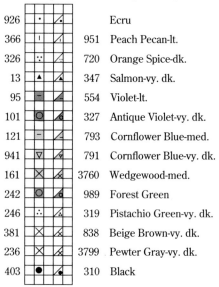

Anchor		DMC	
926			Ecru
366		951	Peach Pecan-lt.
326		720	Orange Spice-dk.
13		347	Salmon-vy. dk.
95		554	Violet-lt.
101		327	Antique Violet-vy. dk.
121		793	Cornflower Blue-med.
941		791	Cornflower Blue-vy. dk.
161		3760	Wedgewood-med.
242		989	Forest Green
246		319	Pistachio Green-vy. dk.
381		838	Beige Brown-vy. dk.
236		3799	Pewter Gray-vy. dk.
403		310	Black

Step 2: Backstitch (1 strand)

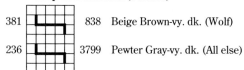

Anchor		DMC	
381		838	Beige Brown-vy. dk. (Wolf)
236		3799	Pewter Gray-vy. dk. (All else)

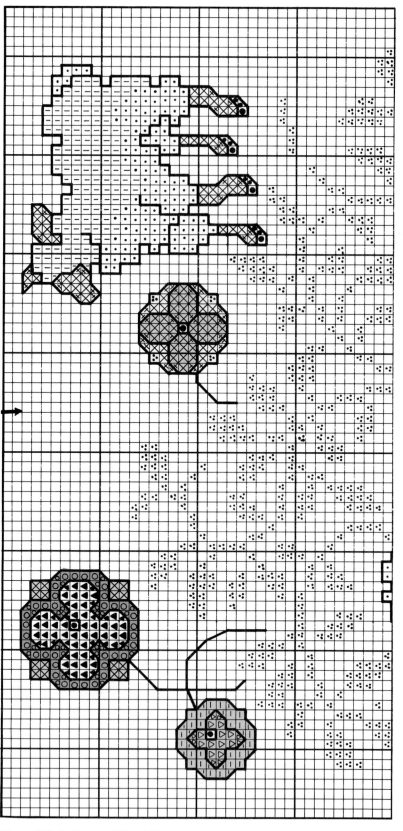

Top • Stitch Count: 78 x 114

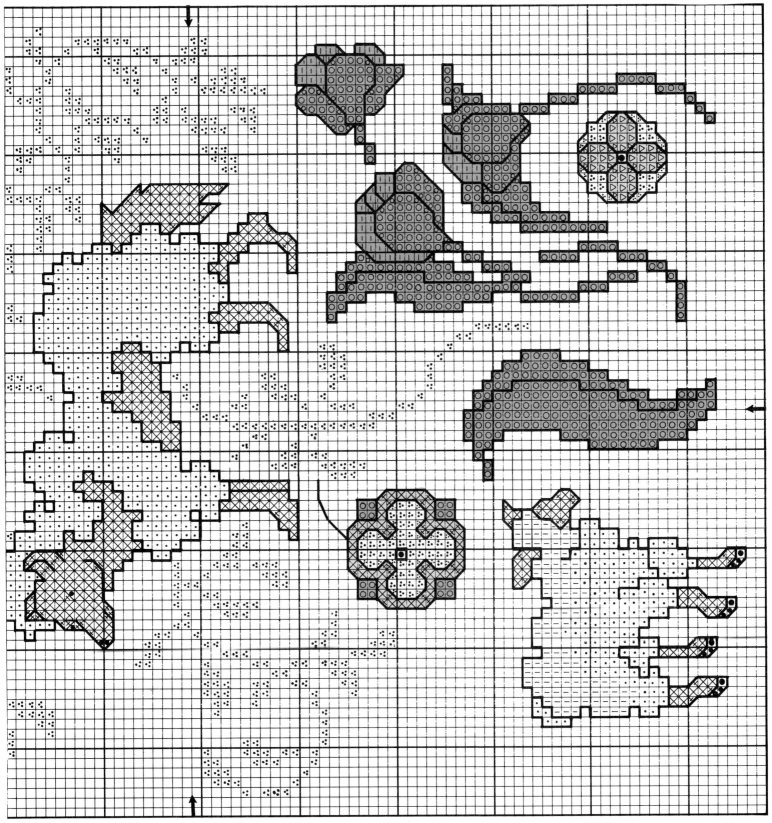

Bottom

The Tortoise and the Hare

The Tortoise challenged the Hare to a race to a tree by the river. The Hare laughed, and as the race began, he ran down the road so quickly that he could no longer see the Tortoise.

There is no need for me to run so fast," he thought. "I will lie in this soft grass and rest for a while." When the Hare awoke, he ran to the tree down by the river, expecting to win the race, but the Tortoise was there waiting for him. Slow and steady wins the race.

The Tortoise and the Hare

SAMPLE
Stitched on Antique Blue Linen 32
over two threads, the finished design size is
6¼" x 3¾". The fabric was cut 12" x 10".
Frame as desired.

Other Fabrics	Finished Design
Aida 11	9⅛" x 5⅜"
Aida 14	7⅛" x 4¼"
Aida 18	5½" x 3¼"
Hardanger 22	4½" x 2⅝"

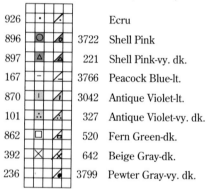

Anchor			DMC (used for sample)	
		Step 1: Cross-stitch (2 strands)		
926	·	╱		Ecru
896	◯	╱	3722	Shell Pink
897	△	╱	221	Shell Pink-vy. dk.
167	-	╱	3766	Peacock Blue-lt.
870	I	╱	3042	Antique Violet-lt.
101	∴	╱	327	Antique Violet-vy. dk.
862	☐	╱	520	Fern Green-dk.
392	✕	╱	642	Beige Gray-dk.
236		╱•	3799	Pewter Gray-vy. dk.

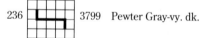

Step 2: Backstitch (1 strand)

236	┗━	3799	Pewter Gray-vy. dk.

Left • Stitch Count: 101 x 59

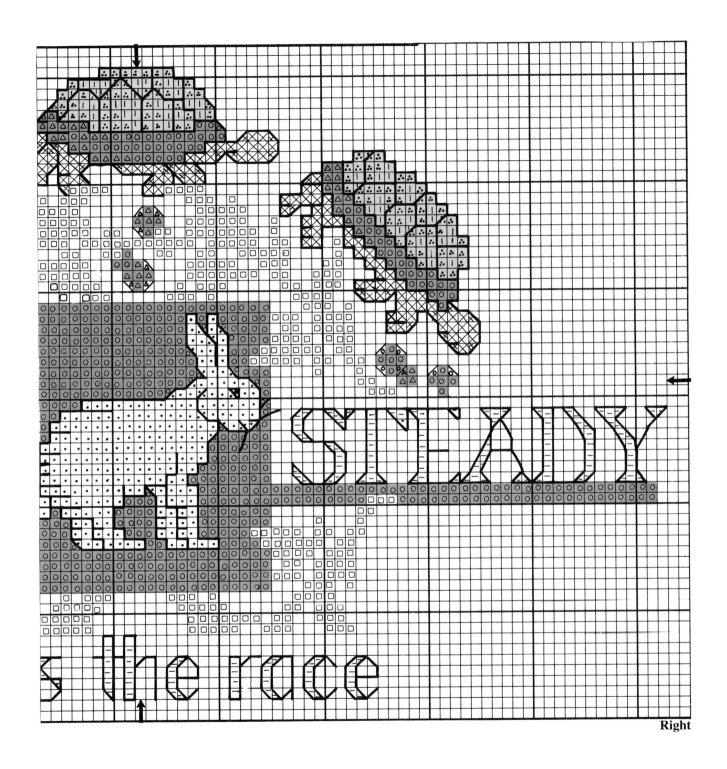

STEADY

s the race

Right

The Country Mouse

Holiday House / New York

THE
country mouse
AND THE
city mouse

A City Mouse went to visit his cousin in the country. The Country Mouse welcomed him to his home, but all he had to offer were corn and grains stored under some dried leaves. The City Mouse said, "Come with me and I will show you how to live."

The two mice set off for town and arrived at the City Mouse's home. They feasted on the remains of jellies and cakes in the dining room. Suddenly, they were chased from the room by a large barking dog. "Better corn and grains in peace than jellies and cakes in fear," cried the Country Mouse as he ran out the door to return to his home in the country.

and City Mouse

The Country Mouse and City Mouse

SAMPLE
Stitched on White Cashel Linen 28
over two threads, the finished design size is
6⅞" x 10⅝". The fabric was cut 13" x 17".
Frame as desired.

Other Fabrics	Finished Design
Aida 11	8⅞" x 13½"
Aida 14	6⅞" x 10⅝"
Aida 18	5⅜" x 8¼"
Hardanger 22	4⅜" x 6¾"

Top left • Stitch Count: 97 x 149

Anchor **DMC (used for sample)**

Step 1: Cross-stitch (2 strands)

Anchor			DMC	
293	○	◢	727	Topaz-vy. lt.
306	□		725	Topaz
890	▲		729	Old Gold-med.
8	▪	◢	353	Peach
10	I	◢	3712	Salmon-med.
13	●	◢	347	Salmon-vy. dk.
95	∴		554	Violet-lt.
98	I		553	Violet-med.
117	▪	◢	3747	Blue Violet-vy. lt.
160	∴	◢	3761	Sky Blue-lt.
168	○		518	Wedgewood-lt.
206	△		955	Nile Green-lt.

Anchor			DMC	
210	✕	◩	562	Jade-med.
363	–	◢	436	Tan
370	◢	◢	434	Brown-lt.
900	·	◢	3024	Brown Gray-vy. lt.
8581	✕	◩	3022	Brown Gray-med.
236		◢	3799	Pewter Gray-vy. dk.

Step 2: Backstitch (1 strand)

236	⌐	3799	Pewter Gray-vy. dk.

Step 3: French Knot (1 strand)

236	●	3799	Pewter Gray-vy. dk.

Top right

139

The Country Mouse and City Mouse

Center left

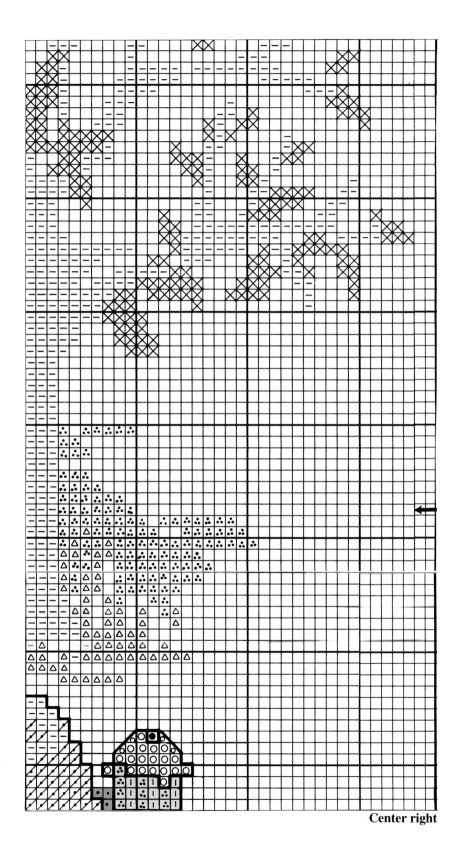

Center right

The Country Mouse and City Mouse

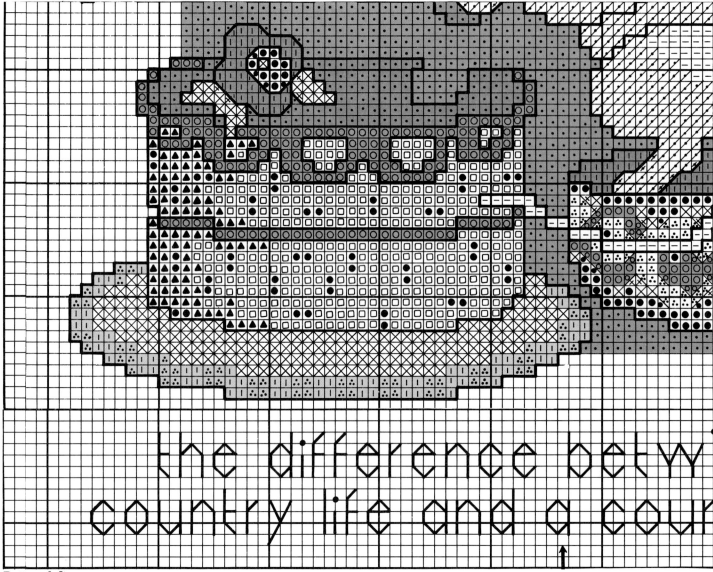

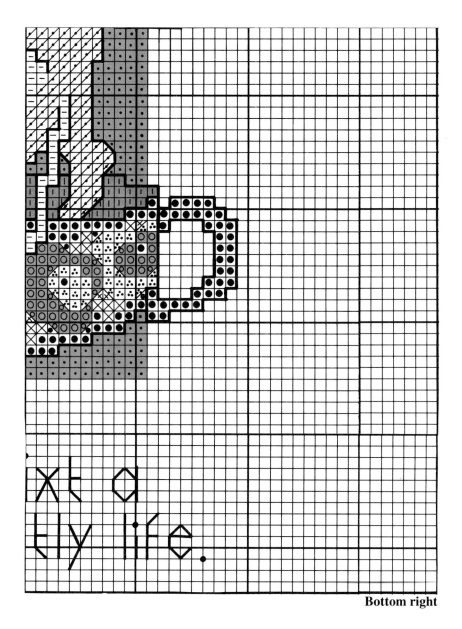

143

Androcles was a poor farmer searching for a fertile area. As he walked, he came upon a lion with a long, sharp thorn in its paw. Androcles pulled the thorn from the lion's paw and continued walking.

The next day, the King's soldiers captured Androcles, thinking him an enemy from another country. Androcles was placed in an arena, and a hungry lion was released from his cage. The lion was the same one that Androcles had earlier helped. The lion recognized him as a friend and licked his hands and face.

Androcles and the Lion

Androcles and the Lion

SAMPLE

Stitched on Confederate Gray Belfast
Linen 32 over two threads, the finished design
size is 6½" x 5¼". The fabric was cut
13" x 12". Frame as desired.

Other Fabrics	Finished Design
Aida 11	9½" x 7⅝"
Aida 14	7⅜" x 6"
Aida 18	5¾" x 4⅝"
Hardanger 22	4¾" x 3⅞"

Anchor   DMC (used for sample)

Step 1: Cross-stitch (2 strands)

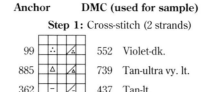
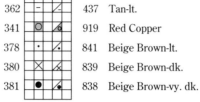

Anchor		DMC	
99		552	Violet-dk.
885		739	Tan-ultra vy. lt.
362		437	Tan-lt.
341		919	Red Copper
378		841	Beige Brown-lt.
380		839	Beige Brown-dk.
381		838	Beige Brown-vy. dk.

Step 2: Backstitch (1 strand)

381		838	Beige Brown-vy. dk.

Step 3: French Knot (1 strand)

381		838	Beige Brown-vy. dk.

Top left • Stitch Count: 104 x 84

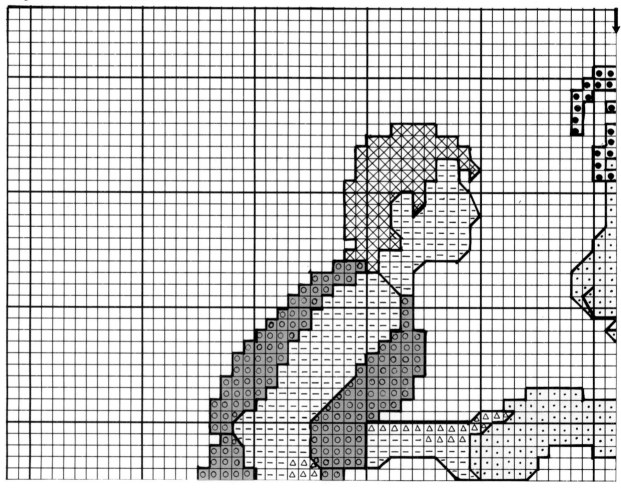

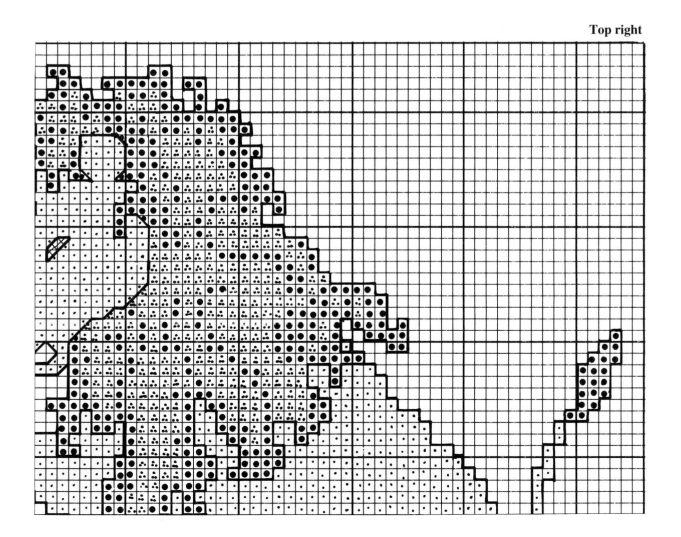

Androcles and the Lion

Bottom left

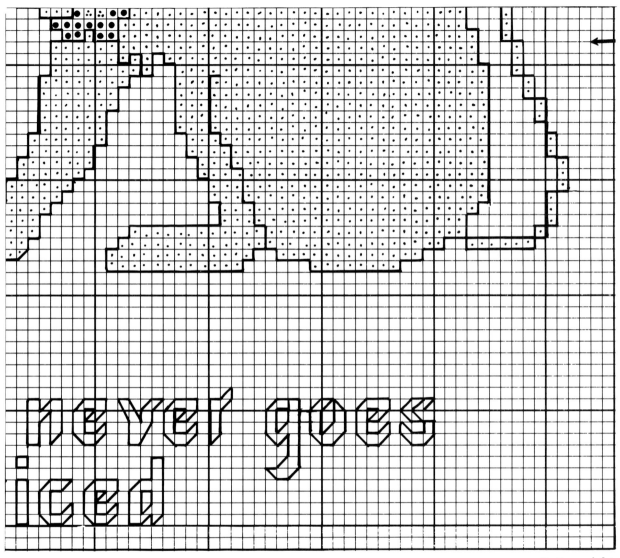

never goes
iced

The Fisherman and

His Wife

A fisherman and his wife lived in a little house beside a river. One day the fish did not bite. He knew that if he did not catch a fish, he and his wife would have nothing to eat.

At last he caught one small fish. As he removed the hook the fish said, "I am so small, I will not make a very big dinner. Throw me back into the water, and when I get bigger, I will make a fine meal."

The fisherman put the fish into his basket and walked back towards his home.

"You may be small," he said, "but a small fish is better than no fish at all."

The Fisherman and His Wife

SAMPLE

Stitched on Antique White Murano 30 over two threads, the finished design size is 9⅜" x 8⅞". The fabric was cut 16" x 15". Frame as desired.

Other Fabrics	Finished Design
Aida 11	12¾" x 12⅛"
Aida 14	10" x 9½"
Aida 18	7¾" x 7⅜"
Hardanger 22	6⅜" x 6"

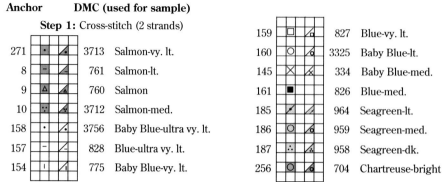

Anchor		DMC (used for sample)
Step 1: Cross-stitch (2 strands)		
271		3713 Salmon-vy. lt.
8		761 Salmon-lt.
9		760 Salmon
10		3712 Salmon-med.
158		3756 Baby Blue-ultra vy. lt.
157		828 Blue-ultra vy. lt.
154		775 Baby Blue-vy. lt.
159		827 Blue-vy. lt.
160		3325 Baby Blue-lt.
145		334 Baby Blue-med.
161		826 Blue-med.
185		964 Seagreen-lt.
186		959 Seagreen-med.
187		958 Seagreen-dk.
256		704 Chartreuse-bright

Top left • Stitch Count: 140 x 133

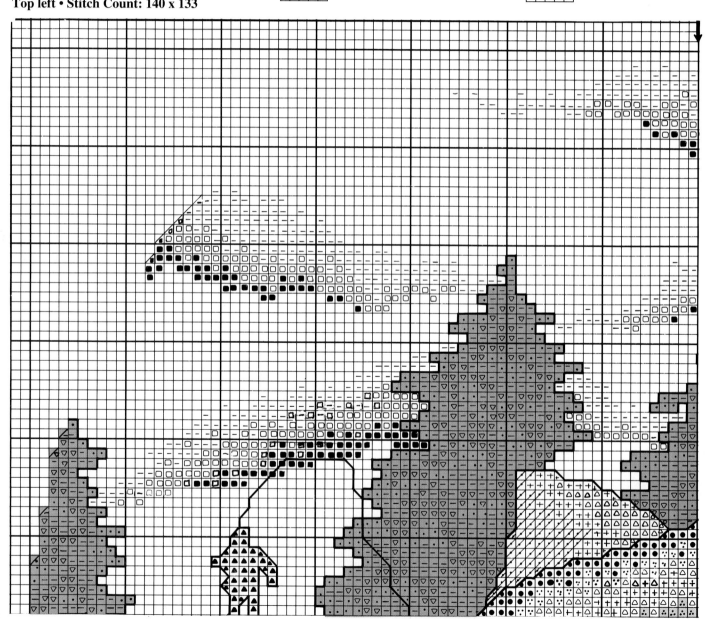

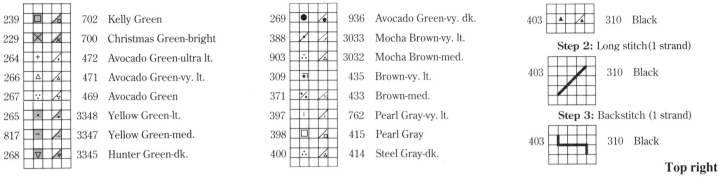

239	702	Kelly Green	269	936	Avocado Green-vy. dk.	403	310	Black
229	700	Christmas Green-bright	388	3033	Mocha Brown-vy. lt.	**Step 2:** Long stitch (1 strand)		
264	472	Avocado Green-ultra lt.	903	3032	Mocha Brown-med.			
266	471	Avocado Green-vy. lt.	309	435	Brown-vy. lt.	403	310	Black
267	469	Avocado Green	371	433	Brown-med.			
265	3348	Yellow Green-lt.	397	762	Pearl Gray-vy. lt.	**Step 3:** Backstitch (1 strand)		
817	3347	Yellow Green-med.	398	415	Pearl Gray			
268	3345	Hunter Green-dk.	400	414	Steel Gray-dk.	403	310	Black

Top right

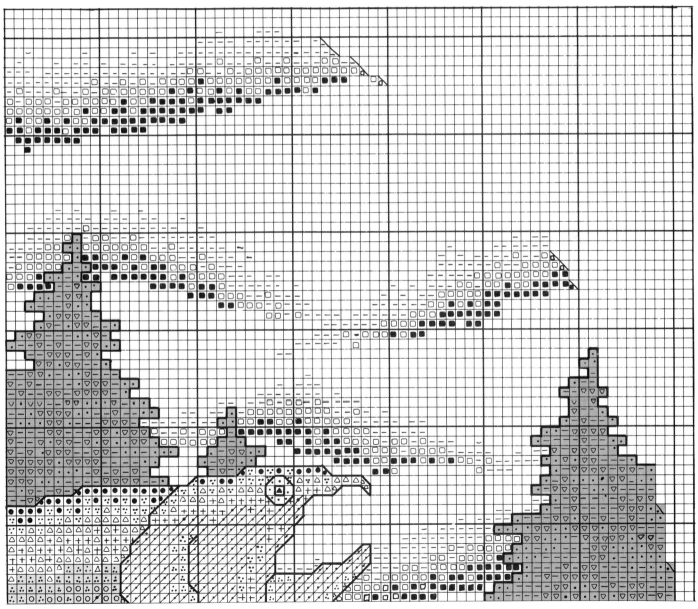

153

The Fisherman and His Wife

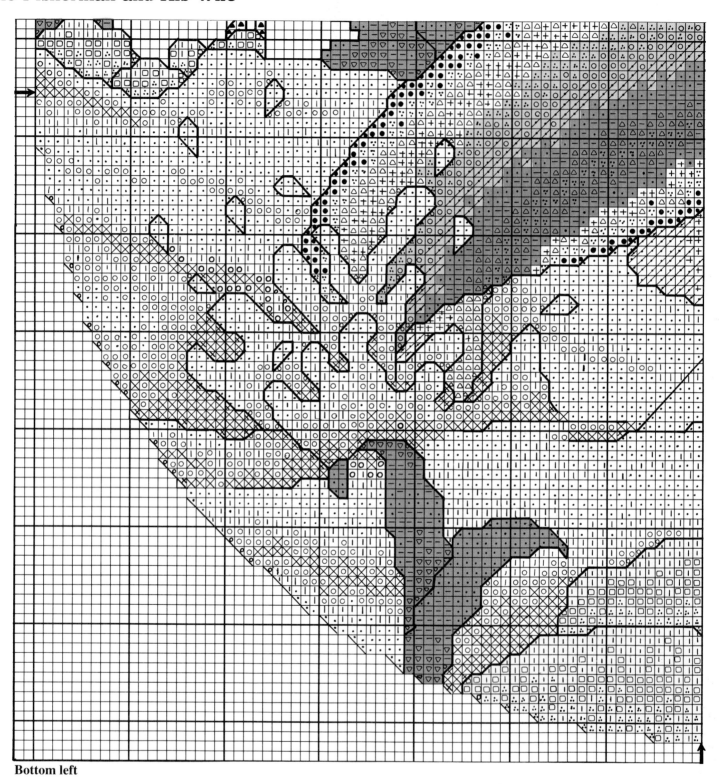

Bottom left

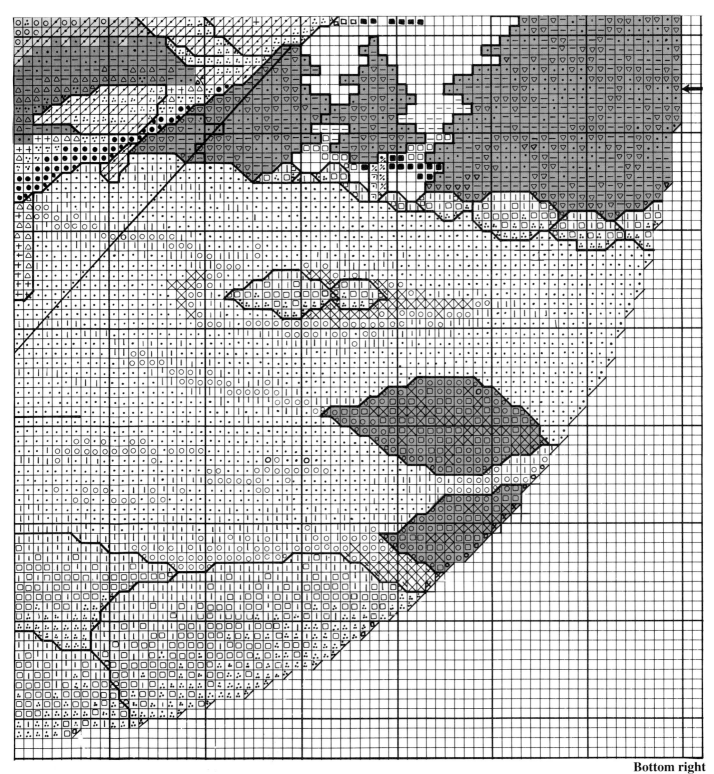

Bottom right

The Leopard and the Fox

A leopard sat in a tree, admiring his beautiful, spotted coat. "I am certainly the finest animal in the forest," he said to himself. A fox passing by overheard him.

"It is too bad you cannot change your spots," he said to the leopard.

The leopard was surprised. "If you had a coat as beautiful, perhaps you would not be jealous," he said.

The fox replied, "I have no spots or glossy finish, but I am content to be the most clever animal in the forest."

There is more to a person than meets the eye.

The Leopard and the Fox

SAMPLE

Stitched on Ivory Murano 30 over two threads, the finished design size is 10⅝" x 10". The fabric was cut 17" x 16". Frame as desired.

Other Fabrics	Finished Design
Aida 11	14½" x 13¾"
Aida 14	11⅜" x 10¾"
Aida 18	8⅞" x 8⅜"
Hardanger 22	7¼" x 6⅞"

Anchor — **DMC (used for sample)**

Step 1: Cross-stitch (2 strands)

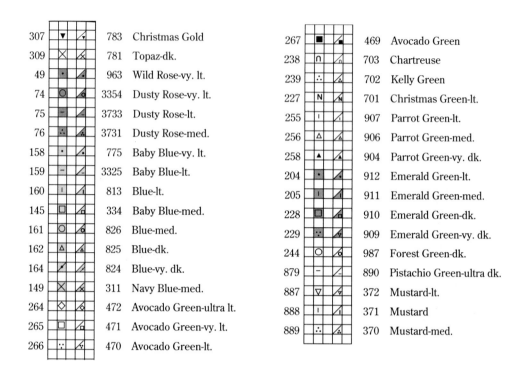

Anchor		DMC	
1			White
293		727	Topaz-vy. lt.
295		726	Topaz-lt.
306		725	Topaz
303		742	Tangerine-lt.

307		783	Christmas Gold
309		781	Topaz-dk.
49		963	Wild Rose-vy. lt.
74		3354	Dusty Rose-vy. lt.
75		3733	Dusty Rose-lt.
76		3731	Dusty Rose-med.
158		775	Baby Blue-vy. lt.
159		3325	Baby Blue-lt.
160		813	Blue-lt.
145		334	Baby Blue-med.
161		826	Blue-med.
162		825	Blue-dk.
164		824	Blue-vy. dk.
149		311	Navy Blue-med.
264		472	Avocado Green-ultra lt.
265		471	Avocado Green-vy. lt.
266		470	Avocado Green-lt.

267		469	Avocado Green
238		703	Chartreuse
239		702	Kelly Green
227		701	Christmas Green-lt.
255		907	Parrot Green-lt.
256		906	Parrot Green-med.
258		904	Parrot Green-vy. dk.
204		912	Emerald Green-lt.
205		911	Emerald Green-med.
228		910	Emerald Green-dk.
229		909	Emerald Green-vy. dk.
244		987	Forest Green-dk.
879		890	Pistachio Green-ultra dk.
887		372	Mustard-lt.
888		371	Mustard
889		370	Mustard-med.

Top right • Stitch Count: 160 x 150

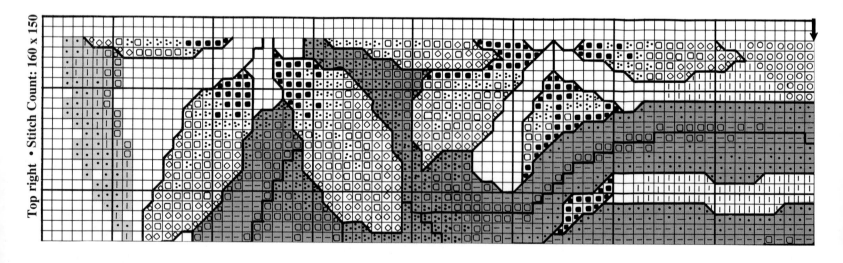

362			437	Tan-lt.
363			436	Tan
309			435	Brown-vy. lt.
370			434	Brown-lt.
376			842	Beige Brown-vy. lt.
378			841	Beige Brown-lt.
379			840	Beige Brown-med.
380			839	Beige Brown-dk.
387			822	Beige Gray-lt.
397			762	Pearl Gray-vy. lt.
399			318	Steel Gray-lt.
400			317	Pewter Gray
401			413	Pewter Gray-dk.
403			310	Black

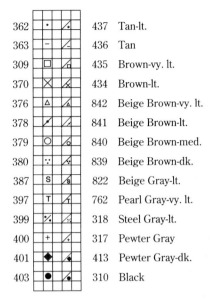

Step 2: Backstitch (1 strand)

403		310	Black

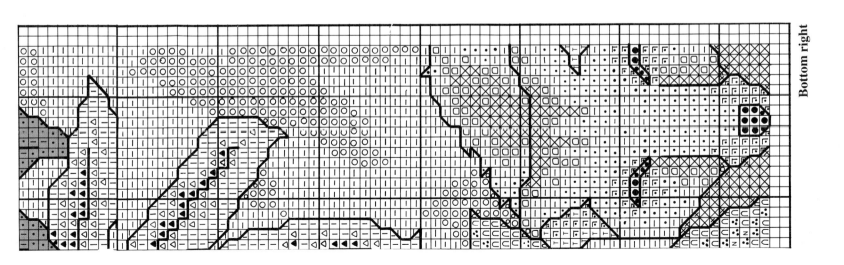

Bottom right

159

Top center

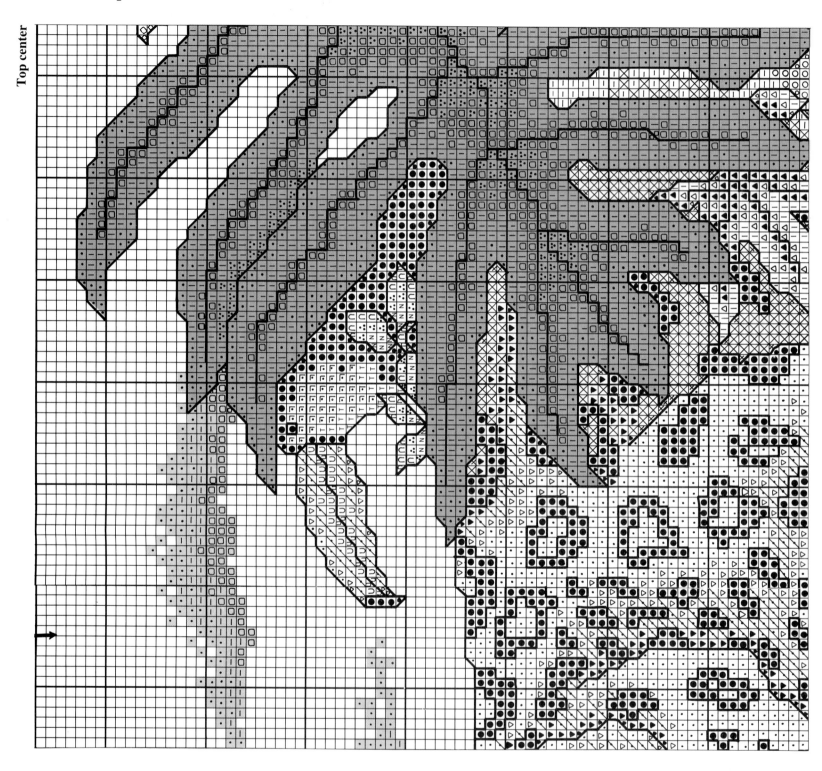

161

The Leopard and the Fox

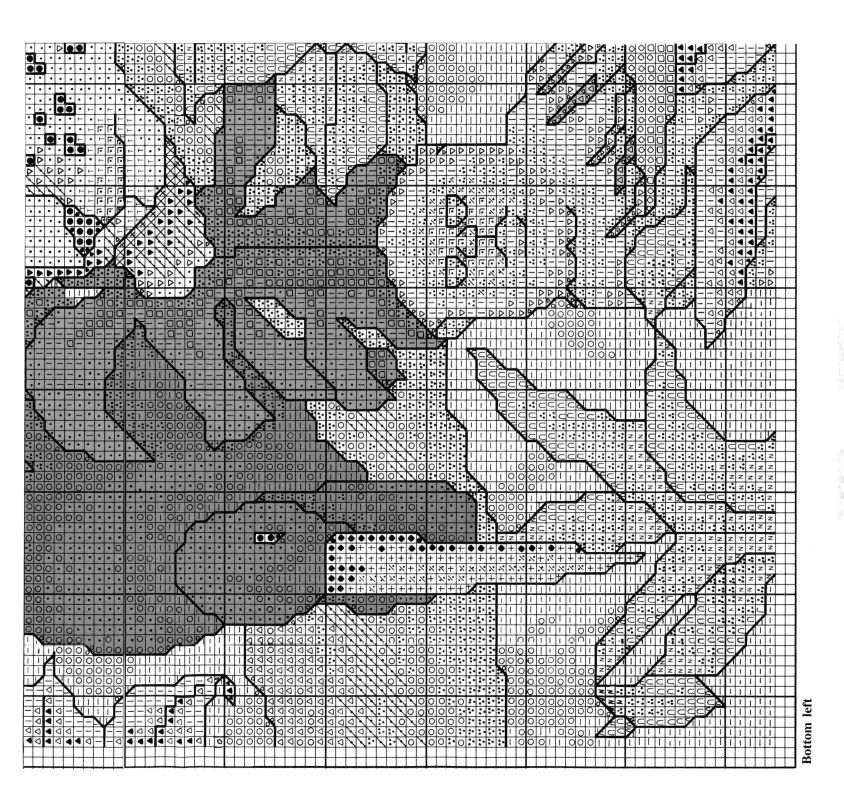

General Instructions for Cross-Stitch

Easy Reference Features

The SAMPLE paragraphs describe the design pieces in each photograph. They also contain any special instructions for stitching or for cutting fabric. When applicable, finished design sizes are also given for other fabrics you may wish to use.

On the graphs, each square containing a symbol represents one cross-stitch and corresponds to a specific thread color as indicated on the color code. The stitch count printed with a graph lists first the width, then the length of the design.

The color codes identify thread by color, number, and brand. The symbols correspond to the symbols on the graphs. The color codes also indicate the kinds of stitches and number of floss strands to use.

Fabrics

Cut the fabric at least 3" larger on all sides than the design size or cut it the size specified in the SAMPLE information. A 3" margin is the minimum amount of fabric required to ensure plenty of space for matting, framing, and other finishing techniques for your stitched piece. To keep fabric from fraying, whipstitch or machine-zigzag the raw edges, or apply liquid ravel preventer and allow to dry. Using a stretcher bar frame or a hoop keeps fabric from wrinkling, ensuring uniform stitches.

Centering the Design

Unless otherwise indicated in the directions, the design should be centered on the fabric. Fold fabric in half horizontally, then vertically. Place a pin in the point of the fold to mark the center. Locate the center of the design on the graph by following the paths of the vertical and horizontal arrows printed on the edges of each graph to their intersection. Begin stitching at the center of the graph and fabric.

Needles

A blunt tapestry needle, size 24 or 26, will slip easily through fabric holes without piercing fabric threads. Never leave a needle in the design area of the work; it may leave rust or a permanent impression on the fabric.

Stitching

Cut thread into 18" lengths; longer pieces tend to twist and knot. Run floss over a damp sponge to straighten. Separate the strands, then use the number of strands indicated in the color code. Thread should lie flat; if it begins to twist, suspend the needle and allow it to unwind.

Secure the thread by inserting the needle up from the underside of the fabric at the starting point. Hold 1" of thread behind the fabric and stitch over it with the first few stitches. Another method for securing thread is the waste knot. Knot the thread and bring the needle down through the fabric about 1" from where first stitch will be. Work several stitches over the thread to secure. Cut off the knot later. To finish thread, run it under several stitches on the back of the work.

To carry thread, weave it under previously worked stitches on the back of the design. Do not carry thread across fabric that is not or will not be stitched. Loose threads, especially dark ones, will show through.

Beadwork

Cross-stitch all non-beaded areas of design before doing any beadwork. Apply each bead in the same manner as a cross-stitch (see Diagram on opposite page): stitch from lower left to upper right, passing floss through bead; bring needle up again at lower right, pass through bead again, and insert at upper left. When working in rows, first make all left-to-right diagonal stitches in the row, then return to secure beads with the right-to-left diagonal stitches.

Cleaning Completed Work

Soak finished design piece in cold water with mild soap for 5-10 minutes; rinse. Roll in a towel to remove excess water; do not wring. Place face down on a dry towel and iron on a warm setting until dry.

Stitches Used

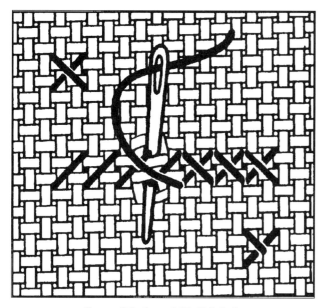

Cross-Stitch and Half Stitch

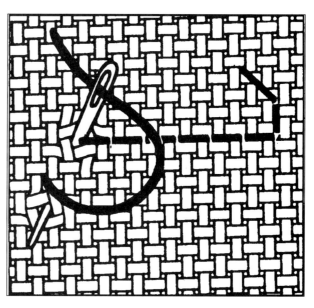

Back Stitch

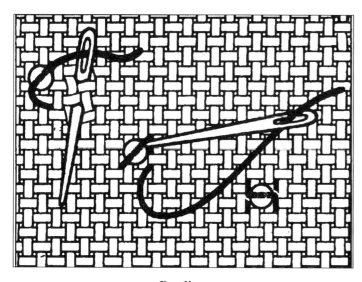

Beading

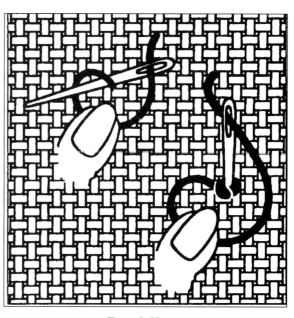

French Knot

General Instructions for Pillows

Bias Strips

Cut fabric square in half diagonally (along the bias). Beginning at one 45-degree corner, fold fabric several times (see Diagrams below), aligning bias edge, until opposite corner is met. Cut strips of required width for binding or piping, parallel to bias edge. For ¼" piping, cut strips at least 1" wide; for ⅜" piping, at least 1¼"-wide strips are required. Join strip ends along straight grain to make a longer strip of required length.

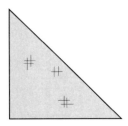

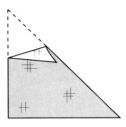

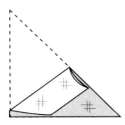

Mitering Corners

After pillow center is completed, stitch on any border strips, beginning and ending at the adjacent seam allowances. Backstitch. Fold two overlapping border strips or fabric corners together at a 45-degree angle, as shown in Diagram. Mark both sides; pin and then sew on marked line. Trim seam allowance to ¼". Repeat for all four corners.

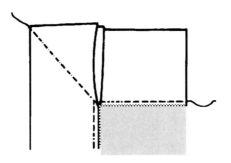

Corded Piping or Ruffles

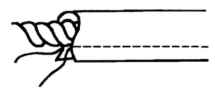

To make piping, encase a length of cord in a pieced bias strip and stitch as closely as possible, using a zipper foot. To attach piping or ruffles, pin around right side of pillow front, beginning at center of one edge, so that stitching line of piping or ruffle lies on seam line and flat/apron edge of piping is inside seam allowance. Stitch up to seam allowance of adjacent edge: Pivot with needle in fabric at corner. Clip flat/apron edge of piping up to seam line. Continue stitching next edge.

To finish ends of ruffle (if not already joined), leave about 1" free when starting place is reached, make neat seam across ruffle ends, finish stitching ruffle to pillow.

To finish ends of piping, remove 1" of stitching at each end of bias strip. Fold under ¼" of fabric at one strip end; lap raw end over folded end. Trim cord so ends butt. Whipstitch piping ends together and refold bias strip. Finish stitching to pillow.

Finishing

Once the front of the pillow has been completed, place it on top of the backing, right sides facing together. Sew the two pieces together, leaving a 3"-4" opening for turning and stuffing in one side. Turn pillow right side out through the opening; stuff, then slipstitch the opening closed.

Suppliers

Fabric

Zweigart/Joan Toggitt Ltd.
Weston Canal Plaza
2 Riverview Drive
Somerset, NJ 08873
(908) 271-1949

Antique White Belfast Linen 32
Confederate Gray Belfast Linen 32
Cream Belfast Linen 32
Light Mocha Belfast Linen 32
Platinum Belfast Linen 32
Sand Belfast Linen 32
White Belfast Linen 32
Amaretto Murano 30
Antique White Murano 30
Ash Rose Murano 30
Cream Murano 30
Ivory Murano 30
Pewter Murano 30
White Murano 30
White Cashel Linen 28

Wichelt Imports, Inc.
RR1
Stoddard, WI 54658
(608) 788-4600

Antique Blue Linen 32
Delicate Teal Jobelan 28

Floss and Beads

Floss
The DMC Corporation
Contact:
American Needlewoman
(800) 433-2231
Herrschner's
(800) 441-0838

Mill Hill Beads
Gay Bowles Sales, Inc.
P.O. Box 1060
Janesville, WI 53547
(608) 754-9466

032HL Balger Pearl Blending Filament
017HL Balger Blending Filament
Kreinik Mfg. Co, Inc.
P..O. Box 1966
Parkersburg, WV 26101
(800) 537-2166

Kits and Accessories

Polyester stuffing
Fleece
Fairfield Processing Corp.
P.O. Box 1157
Danbury, CT 06813-1157
(800) 243-0989

#912 Box with insert top
Freeman & Co.
416 Julian Avenue
Thomasville, NC 27360
(910) 476-4936

Clock
Sudbury House
Box 895
Old Lyme, CT 06371
(203) 739-6951

Index

Alphabets and Numerals 80-81

Androcles and the Lion 144

Androcles and the Lion code 146

Beadwork 164

Bias strips 166

Cat and the Fiddle 60

Cat and the Fiddle code 62

Centering 164

Cinderella 40

Cinderella code 42

Cleaning 164

Corded Piping 166

Country Mouse, City Mouse 136

Country Mouse, City Mouse code 139

Cow Jumped Over the Moon 60

Cow Jumped Over the Moon code 64

Cross-stitch diagrams 165

Cross-stitch General Instructions 164

Fabrics 164

Fisherman and his Wife 150

Fisherman and his Wife code 152

Frog Prince 28

Frog Prince code 32

Goldilocks 16

Goldilocks code 18

Goose and Golden Egg 116

Goose and Golden Egg code 118

Goose and Golden Egg pillow 118

Hansel and Gretel 22

Hansel and Gretel code 24

Jack Sprat 82

Jack Sprat code 84

Leopard and the Fox 156

Leopard and the Fox code 158

Little Bo Peep 88

Little Bo Peep clock 90-91

Little Bo Peep code 91

Little Red Ridinghood 10

Little Red Ridinghood code 12

Mary, Mary 100

Mary, Mary code 102

Mitering Corners 166

Needles 164

Old Woman in a Shoe 106

Old Woman in a Shoe code 109

Old Woman in Shoe photo album 108

Pillow finishing 166

Pillow General Instructions 166

Princess and the Pea 34

Princess and the Pea code 38

Princess and the Pea pillow 36

Rapunzel 46

Rapunzel code 48

Ring A Ring O Roses 66

Ring A Ring O Roses code 68

Rock-a-Bye Baby 74

Rock-a-Bye Baby alphabets 80–81

Rock-a-Bye Baby code 76

Ruffles 166

Rumplestiltskin 52

Rumplestiltskin code 56

Rumplestiltskin pillow 54

Stitching 164

Tortoise and the Hare 132

Tortoise and the Hare code 134

Twinkle, Twinkle 94

Twinkle, Twinkle box 96

Twinkle, Twinkle code 98

Wind and the Sun 122

Wind and the Sun code 124

Wolf in Sheep's Clothing 128

Wolf in Sheep's Clothing code 130

All of us at Meredith® Press are dedicated to offering you, our customer, the best books we can create. We are particularly concerned that all of our instructions for making projects are clear and accurate. Please address your correspondence to Customer Service, Meredith® Press, 150 East 52nd Street, New York, NY 10022.

If you would like to order additional copies of any of our books, call 1-800-678-8091 or check with your local bookstore.